DEISM

Grace's Search for the Truth

David ben Avram, PhD

Amizakai baht Miriam, PhD

Kfar Golem Productions

Israel

Cover Design by Amizakai baht Mariam, PhD

1st Edition

CHAPTER ONE

FALLING GRACE

"Come in Thelma," said Doctor Phelps, the staff psychiatrist of The Berlin Institute of New Hampshire.

Thelma Akin, the staff psychologist, took a seat at the small conference table in Phelps' office. She placed a file on the table and unfolded it.

"You talked to Sharp this morning?" asked Phelps.

"First thing," replied Thelma.

"So, give me a run-down. I practically know the story from cable television," said Phelps.

"Well," began Thelma, "she belongs in here and my first impression is that this is going to take a while. Let me start from the beginning. Grace Sharp, that is Doctor of Divinity Grace Sharp, was born in Tulsa, Oklahoma on 17 August 1958. Nothing to note in her childhood that would cause her to be motivated by any past pain. Except that is, her resent crash. Her father was a minister with quite a large following. They lived well. Grace did not want for anything. Grade school, high school, Oklahoma State University, all top grades. She went to seminary in North Carolina, All Believers University, back when the Right Reverend Bishop Elgood Twain was the chancellor."

"Is still doing time, if I remember correctly," said Phelps.

"All Believers almost went under. They got lucky and the staff was able to talk Doctor Marshall into taking the reins. This was all going on when Grace was attending. She told me she did worry about her tuition going up in smoke after Twain walked off with so much of the money. Anyway, she graduated in 1979 and returned to Tulsa to serve in her father's ministry. Reverend Sharp started a local television mission and his hour-long shows were soon syndicated, and he went nation-wide. Grace joined him in the televangelist business, and she was a natural. But she did take a two-year hiatus to get her doctorate. Thus, we have Reverend Doctor Grace Sharp in our care," said Thelma.

"She ended up with her own show as I remember, not that I watch televangelists," said Phelps.

"Her success made her a multi-millionaire, but she did not flaunt it … jets … mansions … all that fall-de-rall was not for her. She gave a lot of it away. All of her charity giving was here in the states. I guess she realized that there were enough poor in America, she didn't have to go overseas. And, again, she did not flaunt it. After years in the television ministry, she was offered the top job at All Believers, but she still kept her show, although it was reduced to an hour. And, that led to her becoming the chair of the president's ecumenical council. She was the chair for about three years until she began to doubt her faith. She struggled with that for several years and never told anyone. Her father and mother went to their graves without knowing she was starting to pull away from her 'truth in ministry' as she calls it."

"What caused her to make the break and go public with it?" asked Phelps.

"It was while she was doing one of her shows. She just blurted out that she was failing in her faith. She never went back to her show, left the university and resigned from the president's council."

"Then what?" asked Phelps.

"She told me she was hounded by the public. She got death threats on her home phone answering machine, on her cell, both calls and text messages, and she even got threats via snail mail. Before she signed herself in here, she was a recluse for a year," said Thelma.

"But why here, why us, all this way from Tulsa?" asked Phelps.

"She said she wanted to get as far away as possible," replied Thelma.

"Depressed?" asked Phelps.

"Clinical depression and I believe she may be hallucinating. She is very paranoid. An orderly tapped on my door while I was interviewing her, and she jumped a foot off the chair. The nurse practitioner, the new one on the night shift," said Thelma.

"Louise, Louise Lithwick," said Phelps.

"Louise gave her Klonopin to reduce her anxiety. I think it was brave of her to realize she was falling apart, as she referred to her condition," said Thelma.

"Let Louise decide when to take her off the medication. It's the hallucinations I am worried about," said Phelps. "Did she self-report that?"

"Yes," replied Thelma.

"What do you think?" asked Phelps.

"Right now, she sounds like a good candidate for Vraylar," replied Thelma.

"Okay. I'd like to see her this afternoon, and I would like you to come in with her. I'm open from two on," said Phelps.

"Then two it is. See you then," said Thelma.

The orderly knocked on the window to Grace's room door and stepped in.

Grace was lying on her bed staring at the ceiling.

"You have a two o'clock with Doctor Phelps and its ten of," said the orderly.

"Doctor Phelps?" asked Grace.

"He's the staff psychiatrist. Thelma will be going with you," replied the orderly.

"What's your name?" asked Grace.

"Lorna," replied the orderly.

"Do I really have to go?" asked Grace.

"Afraid so. It is all part of your in-take. It takes 'bout three days for your in-take to be finished and then you get a recovery plan. Doctor Phelps will go over that with you. Gotta get goin'," said Lorna. "I am assigned to this floor and you will see me often. How was lunch?"

"Can't complain about that. I like tacos. Okay, let's go," said Grace.

They took a short walk down the hallway to the elevator and went down two floors to what was known as the psyche floor where all the staff had their offices. Doctor Phelps had his door open. Thelma was already sitting at the conference table.

"Hi, Lorna. Come on in," said Phelps.

Grace stood still in the doorway. Phelps approached her and shook her hand. "Grace, I am Doctor Phelps. Please come in and take a seat at the table next to Thelma. Thanks, Lorna."

Lorna closed the door as she left the office.

"Well, here we are," said Phelps as he took his seat across from Grace and Thelma. "I asked Thelma to be here today as I felt you would be more comfortable. We are meeting as part of the in-take and this is a get-to-know-you session."

"Lorna said it would take about three days," said Grace.

"Usually, sometimes four or five. Thelma and I went over your file. I understand you came here to get far away from Tulsa?" asked Phelps.

"As far away as possible. My last year has been a living hell," replied Grace.

"Let's start off with you telling me how you feel about making that decision," said Phelps.

"I think it was a good choice. I mean … well … I've been treated very well, and I have a private room. As private as one can get with a window in the door. I noticed no men around," said Grace.

"We separate the floors by gender. All the staff on your floor are ladies and they will take very good care of you. Back to how you feel," said Phelps.

"Right now?" asked Grace.

"Yes, right now," replied Phelps.

"Just terrible. I feel I have let so many people down. My audience, the council, the president … everyone," said Grace.

"Guilt?" asked Phelps.

"Up to the hilt with it. As I told Thelma I have gotten a lot of death threats. Some Christians, huh," said Grace. "I lost my faith and they turned against me … turned on me like bull-dogs."

"I am sorry to hear that. I understand you feel as if you have been hallucinating. Tell me about that," said Phelps.

"It feels as if I am talking to myself in a different voice. And the voice is threatening me … just like the threats I received in Tulsa," replied Grace.

"Do you have any visions?" asked Phelps.

"No, no visions. Will I eventually?" asked Grace.

"There is no reason to believe that. Although it could happen. And if it does happen, I want you to tell a staff member right away," said Phelps.

"Am I schizophrenic?" asked Grace. "Can you just get schizophrenia?"

"You can't get schizophrenia. Not like a disease. But, you can develop it. I am not going to jump to that conclusion right now. But I am going to prescribe an anti-psychotic. It is a medication called Vraylar," said Phelps.

"Now I'm psychotic," said Grace.

"No, you are not psychotic, but it may help with the voices you have been hearing. Let a staff member know if you go a couple of days without hearing them. I don't think it is anything you have to worry about. I believe it will pass," said Phelps.

Thelma interjected, "Doctor Phelps and I discussed whether group therapy would be good for you and we think it will. So, at four this afternoon Lorna will take you to a group session. And, feel open to talk about anything you wish to, or at first you may just want to listen. That would be okay. There is a morning group at nine. I think it would be good to attend them both. The first couple days of group Lorna will take you there and then you can go on your own."

"Gonna turn this basket case loose," replied Grace.

"You are certainly not a basket case," said Phelps. "Okay, you are going to be busy with your group sessions and your half hour a day with Thelma. Good. It'll get you out of your room," said Phelps.

"And it doesn't hurt to mix a little with the other guests," said Thelma.

Grace laughed. "I'm a guest."

"Yes. This is an institute, not an institution," said Thelma.

"So, I can leave anytime I want to? asked Grace.

"Yes. You can," replied Phelps.

"Don't need my street clothes just yet. I'm not going anywhere," said Grace. "This is the most secure I have felt in a long, long, time."

"That about does it for today," said Phelps.

"Come with me. I'll take you back to your floor," said Thelma.

"How did your first group go?" asked Lorna.

"Not all that hot," replied Grace.

"Why, what did you share?" asked Lorna.

"Nothing … just listened. But two ladies in the group recognized me. They started to talk about how they loved the show," said Grace.

"How does that make you feel?" asked Lorna.

"I was wondering how long it would be before I was asked that question. Gotta have that question in a cracker factory, don't you?" asked Grace.

"Cracker factory?" asked Lorna.

"I read a book about a woman's experience as a patient in an institution, not an institute. She was a patient, not a guest. Good book," said Grace.

"The floor nurse says you can go to dinner on your own. And right after dinner, you can get your meds. We always issue meds on a full stomach," said Lorna. "Dinner at six, don't forget," said Lorna.

"See you around the campus," laughed Grace as she went into her room.

CHAPTER TWO

GRACE'S GOD

"Grace. Grace."

"Oh my," said Grace to herself as she sat up. "Now I'm talking to myself in my head."

"It's three in the morning, Grace," said the night nurse named Lithwick as Grace was approaching the nurse's station.

"I'm hearing voices. Thelma told me to tell the staff when it happens. Do I get another Vraylar?" asked Grace.

"No, you don't get another Vraylar. But I am going to make a note of it and let Thelma know," said Lithwick.

"I'm sixty years old and falling apart," Grace started to cry.

"It's not all that bad, honey," said Lithwick. "There are many on this floor that have some very tough stories to tell. You are just in a bad place right now. It'll get better."

"Will I have to stay on these medications for the rest of my life?" asked Grace.

"That is up to Doctor Phelps to decide. I can't answer that one. Let me ask you this. Are you hearing the voices less frequently?" asked Lithwick.

"Not really. I've only been on the meds for two days. I guess I shouldn't expect too much," said Grace.

"You have to understand that it takes time for the meds to settle in. Don't expect too much for a while, just remember the voices and let Thelma know so we can log them each time you experience the voices," said Lithwick.

"Nah, that is a lot of trouble. I'll just tell Thelma … plus I don't need to be wondering around all hours of the evening or morning. Okay, I'm going back to bed," said Grace.

"Don't forget group in the morning," said Lithwick.

"Night," replied Grace.

<<<>>>

"Grace. Grace," said a voice.

Grace sat up and looked at the clock on her nightstand. "Maybe if I answer the voice," thought Grace. "What? … it is four in the morning."

"Grace, Grace, you will be refreshed in the morning," said the voice.

"I better be. You are stirring around in my head isn't helping with my sleep schedule," replied Grace. "Who are you?"

"Grace, I'm here to help you," said the voice.

"How is that?" asked Grace.

"You don't believe anymore, but you still have doubts. Am I right?" asked the voice.

"Yes, I do. But I know there is no God, but yet there is that thought of my being wrong rattling around in my head. It won't go away. But then again, I am talking to myself. It brings up guilt and shame for turning my back on the church. I just couldn't lead my flock anymore. I feel I turned my back on them," said Grace.

"You turned your back on something that was not there," said the voice.

"What?" asked Grace.

"God. You are right ... there is no God. There is no God in the universe and we will work together proving that. Trust me," said the voice.

"A voice in my head ... trust a voice in my head? I need another Vraylar," said Grace.

"You don't need anything except to listen and reply," began the voice. "We will have a conversation. And, no one will hear you talking. No one can hear you talking right now. You are just sitting up in your bed. Your mouth is not even moving. We will meet every night and you will learn from me. I have much to teach you, but you will do the teaching. You will do the teaching to prove there is no God in the universe. I will just guide you. You don't even have to sit up to talk to me, but if someone looks in the window in the door, they will not see you sitting up. You will appear fast asleep. So, how does that make you feel?"

"I can't stand hearing that question," said Grace realizing for the first time her lips were not moving. "Suppose I go along with this? This can't be progress for me. It will ... I guess ... after a while that I will be getting worse."

"Hardly. You are strong and will get through this," replied the voice.

"Okay. So, when do we start?" asked Grace. "And who are you? I mean I realize you are just in my brain, but ..."

"That is the topic we will start with ... the brain ... when we really get into it. But first, I have to give you a little introduction to all of this ... this adventure for you. And that will happen tomorrow night. So, you have something to look forward to. And until then, Good night," said the voice.

"Wait, who are you?" asked Grace. Suddenly she felt a calm she has not felt since she realized she had lost her faith. "Okay let's see what happens. Might not help, but it couldn't hurt."

<<<>>>

"Grace, you seem as if you want to share," said Ginny, the morning group facilitator.

"Well ... I don't know ... it may sound bad," replied Grace.

"Whatever it is, it is probably not all that 'bad' as you say," said Ginny.

"Well ... this may sound crazy ... but ... after all look where I am," laughed Grace.

"You are not crazy. There is no medical term such as crazy," said Ginny.

"Okay, I hear voices. I have been hearing voices for about the last year. At first, they were as if a whisper, and I could not understand anything, but I knew they were voices. However, last night I heard a voice and it was loud enough for me to understand everything," said Grace.

"What was the voice saying?" asked Ginny.

"You're not making fun of me, are you?" asked Grace.

"We would never do that in group. We would never do that anywhere in the institute. So, what were you hearing?" asked Ginny.

"He, it was a man's voice. He said he would help me with my loss of faith," said Grace.

"To get your faith back?" asked Ginny. "I'm sorry, I keep interrupting you. Please, go on."

"He said he knew that I was struggling with my breaking with the Lord and could help me and work with me to relieve my pain. We had a conversation about what was to come next. He said he had to give me an introduction to 'all of this'. What he meant by that I do not know. He may visit me again tonight unless they up my Vraylar ... which they said they will not do. I hope they change their minds. Anyway, the voice did not identify himself even though he knew I wanted to know who he was. To tell you the truth, I am torn between the Vraylar and wanting him to come back. I want to know what his 'little introduction' will be, but yet I feel with him in my head, I am getting worse," said Grace.

"Were you told that it may take a little time for the Vraylar to become effective?" asked Ginny.

"Yes, but I feel I can't wait a week or more for the meds to kick in," replied Grace.

"Well, that does it for the morning group. Time's up and thank-you for sharing Grace. Believe me, you have made a breakthrough. See everyone at four," said Ginny.

No one said anything to Grace as they left the room. Grace went back to her room and fell on the bed and started to cry.

"Grace. Grace," said the voice.

Grace looked over at the clock. It was two in the morning. "Who are you?"

"Grace. Grace," repeated the voice.

"Yes, I hear you. You don't have to keep calling my name," said Grace.

"I just wanted to make sure I had your attention," replied the voice.

"Who are you? We can't go on like this unless you identify yourself," said Grace.

"I used to be a big, bad, god. At least people thought I was. Way back then, I was a voice in their heads, also. For the sake of our talks, you can call me the greatest god of Greek mythology. And, I accentuate the word god and mythology. If you will follow along with me, you will understand that there were thousands of gods throughout history. Even before written history, and they are all gone now. I am gone ... Thor is gone ... Ra is gone ... Hercules is gone. All the gods are gone except the one you used to believe in. You just went one god more which you no longer believe exists. You believe in no god in the universe," said the voice.

"The greatest god in Greek mythology is Zeus, is it not?" asked Grace.

"Yes," replied the voice.

"You are Zeus?" asked Grace.

"Okay, call me Zeus if you wish. But remember, I do not exist anymore, never did. I am a gone god." asked Zeus.

"So, Zeus, gone god, when do we get started?" asked Grace.

"Now, properly introduced, I think we can start tomorrow. Oh, and do not share about this anymore. They say they don't use the word 'crazy', but if you keep it up, they will definitely think you are bonkers. We don't need that," said Zeus.

"What if they ask me about the voices?" asked Grace.

"Tell them, 'it's all Greek to me'," said Zeus.

"Funny, real funny," replied Grace.

"Okay, tomorrow night we are going to get real serious. Real serious. Until then, Good night," said Zeus.

"Wait! Wait!" said Grace.

"What is it?" asked Zeus.

"You really are Zeus, aren't you?" asked Grace.

"If you want me to be, as long as you don't think I am a god ... never was ... never existed. Night," said Zeus.

"Good bye," replied Grace.

CHAPTER THREE

DEISM'S GRACE

"Nothing to kill or die for and no religion, too," sang Zeus

"Huh?" said Grace.

"From 'Imagine' by John Lennon," said Zeus.

"Now you are singing rock and roll," said Grace.

'*When you see vast armies surrounding Jerusalem and realize nothing but what is desolate is coming. Those in Judea, must run away, perhaps into the mountains to save themselves for those in the city must be gone, and for those living in the countryside must never come into Jerusalem for it has been written, and it will be fulfilled that revenge is coming. And to those pregnant women, and those with babies at their breasts, will suffer great wrath to them and throughout the land. Many will fall by the sword, and all the nations will be captured, and the goyim will destroy Jerusalem and will be fulfilled by their destruction. The heavens will render signs from the stars and the moon and the planets. The sea will roil and send waves over those falling to the ground with fear and fright from things yet to come to the entire earth. Even the powers of heaven will quake in its coming*', said Zeus.

"Good grief, what is that?" asked Grace.

"You don't recognize it?" asked Zeus.

"Sounds Old Testament," replied Grace.

"You are wrong. You are a doctor of divinity and you don't recognize those verses?" said Zeus.

"It's not Old Testament?" asked Grace.

"No, it is from the Gospel of Luke," replied Zeus.

"I feel ashamed for not knowing that," said Grace.

"Don't be. You never taught from it or preached of it on your television program. Admit it, you only taught the good stuff, the stuff people wanted to hear. You never taught of the death and destruction of the Bible, did you?" asked Zeus.

"No. I knew I was preaching what people wanted to hear. The wrath of God is not for broadcast. If I would have preached that from Luke, I would have lost a lot of audience share. They were not ready for that stuff even though the Bible is replete with it; more than enough. So, why those verses?" asked Grace.

"I wanted to get your attention about what is written by men about God's wrath. You ain't heard nothin', yet," said Zeus.

"Well, good grief, where are we going with all of this?" asked Grace.

"You know the Bible has much destruction in it and it was all written by men. So, you ask, what is this all about? We are we starting our talk about Deism with this quote from Luke? It is to provide you confirmation for the reason you initially started to look for answers or alternatives to your belief system," said Zeus.

"Deism?" asked Grace.

"We will get to that as we move along. The God described in the passage from Luke 21:20-26, by the way, is not the God you thought you knew. It is not the God you preached, thought you knew, loved, and from which was brought comfort to you and your flock," said Zeus.

"No, it is not. Who wants to hear that stuff anyway?" asked Grace.

"So, like many others, for as long as religions have ruled flocks of followers, you believed in your heart that there was a religion or philosophy that was better fit for you and them. A religion with answers to the questions for you and your flock. The God you and your flock were seeking was different from the one you were taught to worship. You thought the writers of the scriptures were presenting you a benevolent God, for it was easy for you to disregard the death, destruction, and wrath. Right?" asked Zeus.

"I am beginning to see what you mean," replied Grace.

"There is so mush cruelty brought to us daily on virtually every communications media with the only difference between what you read in the scripture and what you see on the television is what type of weapons are used to destroy one another. You know these passages are in the Bibles, in the scriptures, no matter what version is used," said Zeus.

"Enough, already," said Grace.

"Oh, but Grace we are just getting started. But when we are finished, your pain will be lifted. My question is this. Do you want to make the journey? Do you want to be spiritually lifted up?" asked Zeus.

"I am terribly frightened right now," replied Grace

"You will become calm as we move along. I promise you that. You are a strong woman. You can do it. You can push through to the other side of your pain. Ask yourself this. What is God's point of offering to followers' desolation, vengeance, wrath, and fear? In that one piece of scripture from Luke, can you find anything that provides you comfort?" asked Zeus.

"No, not at all," replied Grace.

"There is nothing of comfort from those words of God embedded in those destructive words. Most, since few have read the Bible from front to back, are unaware that the scriptures have pages filled with these or similar passages. It doesn't matter whether one practices Judaism, Christianity, or Mormonism; and for hundreds of religions of the world, the scriptures are identical in context. Miracles, punishment, the afterlife, God's power, it's all there," said Zeus. But enough for today. This is a lot for you to mull over."

"I am interested in the Deism you speak of. Why Deism?" asked Grace.

"Let the Uncaused Cause, the First Cause, be a mystery for now. It is not the time to discuss it, but be calm, we will get to it. Don't jump ahead," said Zeus.

"It sounds like you have this all planned out," said Grace.

"That I do, and it is all for your benefit. It is all for your mental health. Your stay here in New Hampshire will lift from you your terrible burden. And, as we proceed, you will understand more and more. This is the beginning of your great enlightenment. Relax, enjoy it. Take it all in. Good night," said Zeus.

<<<>>>

'I will try,' thought Grace. She got up, put on her robe and walked to the nurse's station.

Nurse Lithwick was busy shuffling through files.

"Sorry to interrupt you," said Grace.

"Hey, it's four in the morning. I could use a little interruption," said Lithwick. "Is it anything you need, sweetie?"

"Yes, when I came here I had my lap-top with me and they said it would be stored for me. I need to ask a real big favor. Two favors. One, I need a Bible and two, I would like to use my computer," said Grace.

"The Bible I can manage. As for the computer … well … you will have to ask Thelma about that. You see her at ten thirty, don't you?" asked Lithwick.

"Yes, thanks," said Grace.

"How are you doing in group?" asked Lithwick.

"Real well. I am laying off the God stuff unless someone else brings it up and I am no longer talking about the voices in my head. I decided to keep it between the voices and me for now," laughed Grace.

"That might be a good idea. Talk to Thelma about it, though," said Lithwick. "Now, go get some sleep before breakfast."

"Night, er what's left of it," said Grace.

"You'll have your Bible in a few hours once the orderlies on the day shift get here," said Lithwick. "Night."

"Night," replied Grace.

<<<>>>

Lorna knocked on the door.

Grace waved her in.

"Here is your Bible. Sorry, it took a while to find one. We are a secular institute, but I guess you gathered that?" said Lorna.

"Yes, I have, and this is a very good place for me to be," replied Grace.

"Well, gotta run. See ya," said Lorna.

Grace flipped the Bible to Luke and looked for chapter 21 and read verses 20-26. "Right on," Grace said to herself. She flipped to the front of the Bible to the title page. 'Ricci New Age Version'. Grace never heard of that version. "Ricci, Italian, might be Catholic." She flipped through the chapters and found nothing from the Apocrypha. "Isn't Catholic", she thought. "Zeus, I guess you know what you are doing."

<<<>>>

Having been given her computer. Grace brought up a search engine and typed in 'DEFINE DEISM'. A long list of definitions popped up. "How many can there be?" Grace thought. She read: Deism is the recognition of a universal creative force greater than that demonstrated by mankind,

24

supported by personal observation of laws and designs in nature in the universe, perpetuated and validated by the innate ability of human reason coupled with the rejection of claims made by individuals and organized religions of having received special divine revelation.

Deism takes a philosophical position that a God does not interfere directly with the world. It also rejects revelation as a source of religious knowledge and asserts that reason and observation of the natural world are sufficient to determine the existence of a single creator of the universe.

Deism is an understanding that an Uncaused Cause or First Cause may or may not have created the universe.

Deism is belief in the existence of a supreme being, specifically of a creator who does not intervene in the universe. The term is used chiefly of an intellectual movement of the 17th and 18th centuries that accepted the existence of a creator on the basis of reason, but, rejected belief in a supernatural deity who interacts with humankind.

Belief in the existence of a god on the evidence of reason and nature only, with rejection of supernatural revelation'.

'Belief in the existence of god (First Cause) based solely on natural reason, without reference to revelation.

The belief that god (First Cause) has created the universe but remains apart from it and permits (First Cause's) creation to administer itself through natural laws. Deism thus, rejects the supernatural aspects of religion, such as belief in revelation in the Bible, and stresses the importance of ethical conduct.

"Well, that is about enough," thought Grace.

<<<>>>

Ginny, the group facilitator was about five minutes late. "Sorry, admin stuff, don'tcha know."

"Ginny," said Becca. "Grace and I were talking about losing ones' faith and she told me a little about this thing called Deism. Can we open with that? It is really interesting."

"Grace are you up for that?" asked Ginny.

"Sure," replied Grace. "But I am just getting into it. It is sort of a god without a god. I'll try to explain it as far as I know about it. I just started to read about it this morning."

"Please, continue," said Ginny.

CHAPTER FOUR

GRACE'S JOURNEY BEGINS

"Headed off to bed?" asked Lithwick.

"Yes, more voices," replied Grace.

"Just curious. Do you only hear the voices at night?" asked Lithwick.

"Come to think of it … I do … only at night. Didn't think of that," replied Grace.

"I want you to talk to Thelma about that in the morning. I'll leave a note for her," said Lithwick.

"Okay. Only at night, huh. Well, night," said Grace.

"Night, honey," said Lithwick.

<<<>>>

"Grace. Grace," said Zeus.

"Hello, again," said Grace. "I am ready for you, tonight."

"Good, we have a lot to cover," said Zeus.

"The brain … the bit about the brain you were talking about?" asked Grace.

"Soon. We will get to that soon. But first, how many times since you walked away from it all, have you asked yourself 'What was the point'?" asked Zeus.

"Hundreds ... thousands," replied Grace.

"There is a reason for the scriptures to include passages such as the verses I told you about from The Book of Luke. It is quite simple. For you to keep the faith of your religion, passages such as those verses from Luke serve two purposes for those following the religion. Those verses confirm to the follower, through example, that the God of Luke is the only God to worship and secondly, if you, the follower, were to no longer believe in this God, horrid things will happen to you or anyone else who no longer believes in this one God. These verses or others like them, included in every religion's sacred scripture, confirm that by following the belief system ascribed, you and those in your family and those in your flock are bound to go to heaven. But, if you or any of those who follow your teachings don't practice what is written, they have all been given very descriptive consequences of what will happen to them in the afterlife. To avoid these awful things from happening to them, they must practice those things taught in your religion," said Zeus.

"I agree, so far," said Grace. "Please, go on."

"Now, some questions for you. Have you practiced or attempted to practice everything required of you in your religion because you love the things you are supposed to do?" asked Zeus.

"No, I can't say I have. Sometimes I felt obligated," replied Grace.

"Or, instead, have you been a faithful follower for as long as you have, because of your fear of what will be the consequences to you if you don't," asked Zeus.

"I never thought of it as fear," replied Grace. "But, I can see it could develop into fear."

"You needn't feel remorse for it being felt to be an obligation out of fear. Most have been faithful followers for the same reason. That is the point of religions being practiced today. When you looked into other religions in your years of study, did you find obligations out of fear to be true for each religion?" asked Zeus.

"You keep bringing up fear," said Grace.

"Oh, you ain't seen nothin' yet," replied Zeus. "Also, if you practiced your religion in this manner, out of fear, it may have been that you were confused about your religion for all these years. You knew you had to learn the requirements of your religion and its history. When you started on your journey, you may have been too young. When young, and innocent, you had no reason to question your religion, the religion your family had practiced for generations."

"I am sure you know my father was a minister," said Grace.

"Of course," replied Zeus. "Another enticement of your religion were the benefits to be gained in the afterlife. For Christianity, it is heaven with the pearly gates at the entrance. Beautiful artwork has been created for centuries depicting this wonderful afterlife. But, if you didn't follow the rules, hell was the place to dwell in the afterlife. For eternity. There is also beautiful artwork depicting that most feared, cruel place. But, again, you began to ask, 'What is the point'? Would a God who loves you, even a sinner, have you, reside for eternity, in such a place? Now, maybe, before reading about Deism, you are not so sure, but you have to admit, it has been part of the questioning of your religion. Before discussing this further, just think of how this one concept of Christianity is repeatedly reinforced in the Christian faith. You do good, you go to heaven. If not, you go to hell. Have you then, all of your life, been a good person to avoid going to hell? So, you have lived a life on Earth because you are afraid of going to hell when you die. That's an awful way to live, isn't it? But you are not alone. Just think of the millions of Christians who believe this and practice their faith solely out of fear? When all they really have to do is treat others as they wish to be treated."

You are now talking about what tears me apart the most," said Grace.

"I think we have had enough for tonight. Except, that is, for one more thing," said Zeus.

"And what is that?" asked Grace.

"Get on that computer of yours and look up reveled religion, faith, and belief. Many of the definitions of Deism began with belief and those belief definitions are wrong. But you will see. Sleep well. And don't forget to go to group," said Zeus.

"Night," replied Grace.

<<<>>>

"Welcome to the morning group. Becca, you don't have to share at first. Perhaps you want to get settled in," said Ginny.

Becca nodded her head.

"Okay, who wants to go first?" asked Ginny.

"I will," said Doris.

"Go right ahead," said Ginny.

"Well, I know we are not to cross talk. Maybe this isn't cross talking, but Grace was sharing yesterday, and she was talking about her losing faith. I have never had any faith. I just don't believe in all that stuff. It all seems so convoluted. I mean raising the dead, and turning water into wine, and the big one, walking on water. I don't mean to turn our talks into religious sessions, but I am so curious how someone can be a Christian school president, on the council for the president, and be one of the most popular televangelists and boom, give it all up? I am very curious as to why one would turn their back on all that money? Hell, I would have just faked it and plodded on for the bennies." said Doris.

"Grace, any comments?" asked Ginny.

"The biggest, most popular, most recognized, and a pastor to presidents lost his faith, but continued on. Only, in his waning days, did he admit it. He was a phony. I am not a phony. For a while, I had doubts, but they were not strong enough for me to quit. But then ... well ... it seemed to hit me all at once. I was becoming a phony. And when I realized that, I quit. I am now trying to understand the reason why. At night I think about it. I am still in the denial phase. Maybe or maybe not, in the denial phase. It is sort of like grieving. Kubler-Ross in her book 'On Death and Dying' listed five stages of grief; denial, anger, bargaining, depression, and acceptance. You don't necessarily go through them in any order. I am struggling with denial, but deep down inside I know I have lost my faith. I just have to prove it to myself. But the phase I am in now is depression, or I wouldn't be here. I'm depressed, or I wouldn't be on Vraylar. I have had my prescription doubled since I have been here … the voice in my head, don'tcha know," laughed Grace.

<<<>>>

Grace remembered that Zeus told her to look up faith and belief. She punched on her computer and typed in 'DEFINE FAITH". Two definitions came up.

'Complete trust or confidence in someone or something.'.

'Strong belief in a god or in the doctrines of a religion, based upon spiritual apprehension rather than proof'.

Then Grace typed in 'DEFINE BELIEF'. Two definitions came up.

'An acceptance that a statement is true or that something exists'.

'Trust, faith, or confidence in someone or something'.

'Faith and belief are the same thing.' thought Grace. "Hmm."

<<<>>>

"Grace. Grace," said Zeus.

"Where were you last night?" asked Grace.

"Hey, even an un-god has to have some time off. Don't worry, you are my only, as they call it here, 'guest'," said Zeus. "You know Christianity is a mean religion. To threaten people with eternal damnation is a very serious matter. Of course, none of it is real. A more poignant example of doing good while living on earth or facing the consequences in the afterlife can also be quite gruesome in other religions," said Zeus.

"What other religions?" asked Grace.

"We'll get into that. Look how many wars America has fought thinking God was on the side of the righteous; America. Remember the old mantra 'kill a commie for Christ'? "replied Zeus."

"I do," replied Grace.

"In fact, unfortunately, because of so many not understanding, many became afraid of you," said Zeus.

"Afraid. Afraid of me. Why?" asked Grace.

"Because of what you taught from the pulpit ... from the television. It was a way for you to get them to continue practicing the religion. It is all the same ... Judaism, Christianity, Mormonism, and on and on. Each takes the position that their revealed-religion is the one, even if it means killing in the name of the religion. Does God want this for us, for us to be afraid of each other? Some would answer 'yes'. All of the revealed-religions are practiced out of fear. If all of this seems, right now, to be logical to you, to ask some of these questions about God, your mindset about religion has grown. Your mindset has grown beyond billions who practice a revealed-religion. Why and how? By understanding our evolution. You question, perhaps your search for another creator, is, what is the point of one god telling people to do horrible things to those that are raised to believe in another god?" asked Zeus.

"But Christianity doesn't do that," said Grace.

"It doesn't? It condemns everyone to hell that does not accept Christ as a personal savior. Few, dare ask the question, 'what is the reason'? You'll be surprised to learn that it is the way our brains have been hard-wired for millennia that we believe what we believe and do what we do in the name of a god. This hard-wire in our brain can be a brain-washing. Sometimes it is easy to do, like raising a daughter to believe in the god of her minister father. That's how people end up being a Christian, or a Jew, or a Mormon. Really, you didn't choose your religion. You were born into the faith, into the culture, into the religion that until a short time ago, you practiced. Now, you are questioning it all. It is in your DNA to believe. Hard-wired and live-wired to believe in a god or gods," said Zeus.

"Gods?" asked Grace.

"As Hindus and Mormons do," replied Zeus. "Well, that is enough for you to think about for today. Rest well. Good night."

"Good bye," replied Grace.

<<<>>>

"So, how are the voices going?" asked Thelma.

"Not really voices. One voice. A male voice. He calls himself Zeus," said Grace.

"Do you talk to him?" asked Thelma.

"Yes, and he talks to me," said Grace.

"I hate this question, but I have to ask it … "

"How does that make me feel?" interrupted Grace, laughing. "Well, Zeus quoted some Bible verses from Luke that I was unfamiliar with. I looked up the verses and he was right on to the tee."

"Are you sure you weren't remembering it, and just thought you forgot it?" asked Thelma.

"No, and let me tell you why," began Grace. "When I taught from Luke, it was normally during the holidays. For the lack of a better term, I cherry-picked what I talked about. It was mostly heaven, and very little hell. I didn't want my ratings to go down with a lot of fire and brimstone."

"Do you talk about this in group? By the way, what is said in group stays in group unless someone threatens to harm themselves or others. That has to be reported," said Thelma.

"I have mentioned my 'voice', but I do not get too deep into it. Several group members recognized me from my show and they wonder how one day I had all that faith, and then lost it. But, and this is a big but, I am still hanging on to a useless belief. I can't let go. Zeus is helping me to understand it all, and he says we are just getting started," said Grace.

"When does Zeus appear in your consciousness?" asked Thelma.

"You mean, when does the voice appear in my head? Zeus comes to me while I am sleeping. I do not wake up, and I don't lose any sleep. I wake up very refreshed. But, it is not like a dream that one forgets soon after waking up. No, Zeus, that is, everything Zeus has said to me sticks with me. Every word," said Grace.

<<<>>>

"Grace. Grace," said Zeus.

"Yes. I am ready," replied Grace.

"I have a bit of news for you. Are you ready to hear what others of your former revealed-religion would consider blasphemy?" asked Zeus.

"Please, continue," replied Grace.

"All that you have learned and practiced from childhood or even with respect to the religion you have recently practiced is nothing but stories about people who never walked the earth. More difficult for you to accept, at first, than Deism, is that billions of people all over the world who are devout followers of their religion have it all wrong. There is no Yahweh, God, or a Mormon celestial heaven dweller. More about that later. Further, most difficult to accept, but what you will eventually understand, is that once you learn about Deism, you'll realize there is no need to go to the tallest mountain to shout out to the world that you have come to understand Deism. There is no god there to hear you," said Zeus.

"Interesting," said Grace.

"What we are embarking upon in these conversations is to prove to you that there are no gods in the universe. You still linger with a touch of belief. This may seem as if it is a difficult task, but the lingering will subside. The Jewish Tanach, or what is known as The Old Testament to Christians, The New Testament, and The Book of Mormon are all convincing to believers, but I submit there is no god in the universe. It is in the writing of those scriptures that proves revealed-religion, which, as you know, is religion based upon divine revelation rather than reason. It is the lineage of mythology. The scriptures have been based upon mythologies passed down over millennia. The scriptures are not divinely written, they are the written word of humans. As seen in the quote from Luke, revealed-religion can be filled with desolation, vengeance, wrath, and fear. Yet, masses of this world's citizens believe and have faith in such writings. There are many supposed gods, but we will key upon five: God of The Tanach, the Christian God in three parts the Father, the Son, and the Holy Ghost. After that, we will discuss the three Gods of Mormonism, as they consider the Father, Son, and Holy Ghost to be three separate Gods," said Zeus.

"Three Gods ... Mormonism? I never knew that," said Grace.

"Yahweh, and God are all created in our hard-wired brains from thousands of years ago, when the myths began leading into the written word around 3000 BC," said Zeus. "I think that will be enough for tonight. Let it all sink in. And, from now on, I will appear regularly. You can count on it. Good night."

"Good bye," replied Grace.

CHAPTER FIVE

RIGHT BRAIN/LEFT BRAIN

"Grace. Grace," said Zeus.

"Good morning," replied Grace.

"Now, we are starting into how revealed-religions came about. But first, a quote from Einstein, 'God does not play dice with the universe.' This quote has been greatly misunderstood over the years. It was believed that Einstein was a religious person; he was not. People assume he had given up physics, again; not true. Einstein did not have a god. He was a Deist and was referring to a god that did not influence the universe after it was created. He said this about his quote being misunderstood, 'It was, of course a lie what you read about my religious convictions, a lie which is being systematically repeated. I do not believe in a personal god, and I have never denied this, but have expressed it clearly. If something is in me which can be called religious, then it is the unbounded admiration for the structure of the world so far as our science can reveal it'," said Zeus.

"I never thought of Einstein in that way. I too, misinterpreted the dice quote," said Grace.

"It was Einstein that presented the world with the idea of a scientific First Cause or an Uncaused Cause. Now, let's go way back to Plato and Aristotle. They both arrived at the idea of First Cause as the creator of the universe," said Zeus.

"I thought you said Einstein did that?" asked Grace.

"Plato and Aristotle did so philosophically. Einstein did so with science. Those two Greeks posited that the universe had a cause for its existence. Maybe a little scientific. It was as good as it was going to get for the 4th and 3rd centuries BC," said Zeus.

"What about the big bang theory?" asked Grace.

"That is just a theory. To believe that our universe, expanded into what it is today, from a pea sized element is a bit far-fetched, don't you think?" asked Zeus.

"Far-fetched sounds about right," replied Grace.

"There are three great mysteries of life. How the universe was created? Is there a god or gods? And, what happens when we die?" said Zeus.

"So, you are going to answer those questions?" asked Grace.

"No, they will still remain a mystery when we are finished with our conversation, but that is a long way off. We can, however, come to an understanding of how the universe has no gods in it. So, the only god would be the First Cause or Uncaused Cause. We will raise many questions about reason. Our reasoning will lead you to true Deism. You are a long way off the mark. You still have doubts about your doubts, don't you?" asked Zeus.

"Yes, that is why I am in this place," said Grace.

"This place is a good place for you to be right now. But Deists have to be careful. There are billions of Christians, 18 million Jews, and 15 million

Mormons, not to mention the hundreds of other religions, including Hindus and Buddhists. It would be inappropriate for a Deist to take their faith away from them. Their religion gives them comfort. Deists do not argue theology," said Zeus.

"I was wondering how to approach that very topic. Good advice," said Grace.

"Therefore, be careful of what you speak of in the groups. With Thelma, yes, but not so much in your groups. Especially as for what we are going to start discussing tomorrow night," said Zeus.

"And what might that be?" asked Grace.

"I'll give you a little preview. How schizophrenia created religion. We are going to discuss the brain. And before you ask, it will have a lot to do with leading you toward Deism. Good night," said Zeus.

"Good bye," replied Grace.

<<<>>>

"Grace. Grace," said Zeus

"Zeus. Zeus," said Grace

"Do I have your undivided attention?" asked Zeus.

"Yes, absolutely," replied Grace.

"Good. Let's start off with a few simple definitions. The first is schizophrenia," said Zeus.

"Now I'm schizophrenic?" replied Grace.

"No. No. But, it is very important to our talk about the brain. So, listen up," said Zeus.

"I'm listening," said Grace.

"Okay. Good. Schizophrenia is a severe mental disorder in which people interpret reality abnormally. Schizophrenia may result in some combination of hallucinations, delusions, and extremely disordered thinking and behavior that impairs daily functioning, and can be disabling," said Zeus.

"Understand," said Grace.

"Good. Now, onto the right brain. The right side of the brain controls the left side of the body. The left side of the brain is referred to as the left hemisphere. But we are more interested in the functioning of the right side of the brain, the right hemisphere. The left hemisphere controls the right side of the body. The right hemisphere functions are art awareness, imagination, all creativity, insight, intuition, music awareness, three-dimensional awareness, and holistic thought. You can look at the book 'Schizophrenia for the Ages' for more information, if you choose to do so. Millennia ago, the right hemisphere was affected by what is known as divine hallucinations. You are a right brained person," said Zeus.

"How is that?" asked Grace.

"You have a great deal of empathy for your fellow man. Empathy is a right brain function. Both sides of the brain are connected by the corpus callosum. When man was first developing, the corpus callosum was not as matured. Thus, the functions of each side of the brain were not yet fully connected, and though each side of the brain functioned to control the opposite side, the thought processes were not yet fully developed. Discovered remains of homo sapiens' can be dated back to 200 thousand years ago. It is believed that the right and left sides of the brains may not have been connected. They had no way to communicate or logically think things out. But, the right side of the brain was in development and just not connected, so imagination did exist, and their thoughts were very much as if they were hallucinating. They were hallucinating, and, developed other personalities in their brain's right side; the imagination side. And these other personalities developed into, let's say, spiritual beings as they were not incarnate," said Zeus.

"This is either brilliant or completely bonkers," said Grace.

"Hang in there. Let's move on. The two sides of the brain were not yet fully connected which meant there was really no explanation for what they saw in their heads. Their thought processes were not that sophisticated. So, throughout millennia, the spirits in humans' heads began to evolve as the corpus callosum grew more attached to each side of the brain. But, as to the right brain hemisphere, the spirits remained as they were now hard-wired. Of course, it was that each human had a different spirit in their head," said Zeus.

"That must have been a confused mess," said Grace.

"The evolution is transferable today. That's not to say that everyone who has a belief in a god or gods is schizophrenic or worse, that a non-believer must be mentally ill because of no belief in god. But, believers have kept the gods in their right brains."

"It is bonkers. What you are saying is that believer's brains are not fully developed. I am not about to tell a believer that their brains are not developed. That's horrible!" said Grace.

"I am not asking you to do that, but, can we say definitively that fundamentalists are hard-wired, still, to the god syndrome? Before you answer, listen to me. It is believed that the development of the corpus callosum, that thing that connects the right and left brain, was a very slow process. Ruins from earlier times show humans to still worship the stars and the sun, just centuries ago. They figured out the seasons by tracking the stars. They ascertained that it took the development of 12 months to go full cycle. 12, today, remains one of the most relevant numbers in revealed-religions. Added to the religion, now dictated by the sun and the stars, humans needed to show god or gods how meaningful they were in their lives. Thus, there were human and animal sacrifices to the gods to show them their faith," said Zeus.

"Well, we don't do that anymore," said Grace.

"Not so. Still today, animals are slaughtered in a kosher ritual and some churches handle snakes in their services. This is all part of a continuation of the hard-wire of the right hemisphere gods," said Zeus.

"By what you said ... well ... you want me to believe believers brains are not developed enough, but atheists' brains are. How can you say that?" asked Grace.

"Humans have gone through hundreds of thousands of Gods from 200 thousand years ago. I was not kidding when I said I was an un-god. No one believes in me anymore. You don't believe I am a god and now you are struggling with your own faith to believe no more in the present god. What is to say in another 5 hundred years Christ will be forgotten and the masses will move on to another god?" asked Zeus.

"That is something to think about," replied Grace.

"Of course, all believers are not underdeveloped or schizophrenic. I just used that to make a point. We are all hard-wired to believe in a god or gods," said Zeus.

"Who believes in gods plural?" asked Grace.

"Remember, Hindus and Mormons, but we will get to that much later," replied Zeus. "You have had enough for this morning. Talk to you tomorrow. Good night."

"Good bye," replied Grace.

<<<>>>

"What does it mean to be right brained or left brained? I think I know, but I am not sure," asked Grace.

"Good question. Psychologists do not use those terms. But, basically, if someone is logical and not very creative, they are considered left brained and if someone is creative ... well ... they are considered right brained," said Thelma.

"Is god in the right hemisphere of the brain?" asked Grace.

"Where are you going with this?" asked Thelma.

"Which side of the brain is a god in?" asked Grace.

"We are secular here at the institute," said Thelma. "Belief in a god is a decision people make. Faith can be very strong. Now, one must ask, is god created in the mind? God has yet to be proven by any scientific method. Thus, a god is a creation within each of us. Belief is a creation within each of us. Faith is a creation within each of us. It is creation that determines where a god resides in our consciousness. And, that creative determination that a god exists is in the right side of the brain."

"Is schizophrenia right brained?" asked Grace.

"Yes, mostly," replied Thelma.

"He was right," said Grace.

"Who was right? There are no men on this floor," said Thelma.

"Zeus, my voice," replied Grace.

"Ahh," said Thelma. "Do you remember everything your voice tells you?

"Every last word of it," replied Grace. "We are talking about the brain. I told him what he is telling me is bonkers.

"Bonkers," replied Thelma.

"Yep, bonkers," said Grace.

<<<>>>

"I don't think Grace Sharp is coming along very well. I expected more progress. She doesn't share anymore in the groups, and she talks about these voices … er … rather this man's voice. She has the idea that she is talking to Zeus and that her religious problems will be solved by listening to Zeus," said Thelma.

"Hmm. If you talk to a god, it is prayer. If a god talks to you, it is psychosis," said Doctor Phelps.

"Really, Doctor," replied Thelma.

"I think this might be late on-set of schizophrenia. Is she developing hallucinations about this character she hears? Other than just hearing him. Has she described what he looks like?" asked Phelps.

"I touched on that and she told me she has no physical description. She only hears Zeus' voice. But, the odd thing is, the voice is leading her somewhere. She has come to believe that the voice can help her deal with her loss of faith. She has mentioned Deism a couple of times," said Thelma.

"First Cause … Uncaused Cause … does she know that Deism is not a religion? She may just end up going to another faith. Do you feel she is searching for another faith?" asked Phelps.

"I think she wants to shed herself of any faith. She says this Zeus is going to lead her to Deism by new understandings of a godless universe," said Thelma.

"I can see why she is not sharing all of this. I am going to put her on Risperdal, point five milligrams. One at bedtime, and one in the morning. I'll call the pharmacy," said Phelps.

"It's going to lengthen her stay. Until the script kicks in," said Thelma.

"Couple of weeks, maybe. Keep a close watch on her. Let me know how she is doing. Until the Risperdal kicks in, she could get worse. Let me know," said Phelps.

CHAPTER SIX

IN THE BEGINNING

"Have you been journaling as I asked you to do? Is that it?" asked Thelma.

"Yes, to both, and I want to read something to you that I found on a search engine. It is from 'Belief Put into Writing'. It goes like this." Grace opened her diary. "Belief in god or gods is a belief in an entity that cannot be proven. The fundamentalists often give the argument that it cannot be proven there is no god. Logically and scientifically, though, you cannot prove a negative. So, though not totally understood as to how or why, gods remain resting in the right hemisphere of the human brain. Those gods have been in that hemisphere for ages. So, from legends and myths passed down through millennia, as the way of story-telling, to the scriptures, they are believed to be the word of God today. The gods in the universe, and even in our little world here on Earth, have a great influence upon billions of those that have faith; those that believe. But, others have different, it is believed, conflicting faiths. The non-believers posit that there is no god or gods. The agnostics doubt that there is a god or gods. And, those that understand Deism understand the First Cause, the beginning, has no influence in the universe. And another one."

"Please. Go ahead," said Thelma.

"The writer of 'God and Your Brain', Timothy R. Jennings, MD, posits that belief and proof of a god is a three-legged stool. He states that science, experience, and scripture prove the existence of a god or gods. He states that scripture was written by a god. Well, scripture began almost as soon as the written word was developed. The Tanach, which is transcribed from Hebrew to English, not transcribed from German to English; as with the King's English in the King James Version. There is a great difference as to the King James Version and The Tanach. So, what version did this god write? God didn't. Man did, and Zeus and I are going to talk about that for a while. When it was all created and who or what created it. By it, I mean the universe. Fundamentalists take the position that the Earth was created on 22 October 4004 BC at exactly six in the evening. God did not write that. Some guy came up with it just as some guys wrote the scriptures to all revealed-religions," said Grace.

Good job. Don't miss group. See you tomorrow," said Thelma.

"Good afternoon, everyone," said Ginny. "Who would like to go first?"

"I would," Naomi replied. "It's about my husband and something he discovered. My husband became a Jew while we were stationed on an army fort. There were Jews in his family and after some study, he decided that Judaism was right for him. He was very active in the synagogue. After that state-side assignment, we were reassigned to Germany. Ezra, that is my husband, had no services to go to where we were stationed and became inactive in his faith. Well, … later on in life, Ezra decided to really study The Tanach. He found The Tanach to be very violent, but, thought that God was protecting the chosen people. It wasn't until 23 years later he concluded that

The Tanach was not a document written by God. He also concluded that the first five books of The Tanach known as The Torah or the Pentateuch was not written by the proclaimed author; Moses. It devastated him. He was no longer a believer. That's all."

"Okay, who is next?" asked Ginny.

<<<>>>

"Zeus, Zeus, are you there," asked Grace.

"Yes," replied Zeus.

"So, what is the topic for tonight?" asked Grace.

"Elon Gilad? He wrote, 'Did Moses Really Write the Torah'," said Zeus.

"Noted," replied Grace.

"A quote from Elon, 'Some three and a half centuries BC, Moses went up to Mount Sanai, stayed for 40 days and supposedly, not only came down with the Ten Commandments, but with The Torah fully written. The odd thing about it is The Torah is written in the third person. Someone else wrote the first five chapters of The Tanach, and all the other books in the third person. Plus, Moses would have had to write about happenings in the future, even his death. The rabbis of the Talmudic era did believe that, divinely inspired, Moses wrote The Torah himself, up to the last twelve verses. The Talmud is a collection of Jewish stories and laws from around 400 AD to 600 AD, is second only to The Tanach."

"Twelve verses were written after the time of Moses. Anyway, to continue with Elon's remarks, 'The Talmud preserves a rabbinical dispute about whether Moses wrote those last verses describing his own death, burial, and legacy, 'which is absurd', or whether they were written by his successor, Joshua'. Also, in Genesis 12:6 it states, 'In the land were the Canaanites'. That verse could only have been written about after Moses died, after the Canaanites were taken over by the Israelites. The verses I will quote from now on, from The Tanach, will be from the Ricci Version."

"I will cross-check with the Bible. I have to see the difference," said Grace.

"You will find a huge difference between The Tanach and The Christian Old Testament of the Christian Bibles. And, about this third person thing. Of the 39 books of The Tanach, 28 are written in the third person. The first 15 books are all third person. Of the 11 not in the third person, 10 are in poem or prose form. Only Nehemiah is written in the first person. One must ask, if Moses wrote about himself in the third person, was he a megalomaniac? The third person writings indicate the books were not written by the supposed author. Moses did not write The Torah. Joshua did not write Joshua. Ruth did not write Ruth, and on and on. I will give you an example. In fact, I am going to give you many examples from here on. In Genesis 14:14, it reads, 'When Abram was alerted to his kin being taken, he called together 318, born of his clan, and followed as far as the city of Dan'. The problem is the city of Dan did not exist until 300 years after Moses died. So, Abram entered a city that was not even in existence. If Moses was not the one who authored The Torah, when was it written? The evidence of the contradictory nature of history and doctrine on the pages of The Torah indicates that the documents did not come from a single source. The evidence within the scriptures themselves is that 613 laws were added, even as late as the post-Babylonian captivity."

"I never heard or read about the time-line with the city of Dan." replied Grace.

"The fact is, there is no historical record that there were hundreds of thousands of Israelites enslaved in Egypt. Indeed, no record of a mass migration from Egypt of any peoples or cultures. Simply stated, Moses did not exist, but more about that later."

"Biblical scholars posit that Moses lived between 1,500 BC to 1,300 BC, though Moses recounts events in the first 11 chapters of Genesis that occurred long before his time; such as the creation and the flood. These earliest accounts were handed on from generation to generation in songs, narratives, and poetry." As it is written in biblica.com. How does the author know of the details and accuracy? It is doubtful that those stories, through the generations, stayed very pure. Rabbinical Judaism calculated a lifespan of Moses corresponding to 1391 BC to 1271 BC. Jerome gives 1592 BC, and James Ussher 1571 BC as Moses' birth year. Here's another one, Joshua is the sixth book of The Tanach, yet Job was written 200 years before and is the 18th book of The Tanach."

"Another chronology lists the writing of Job to be unknown. The five books of The Torah are listed as having been written between 1445 BC and 1405 BC. The chronology also listed Psalms to be written before Joshua, yet Psalms is the 19th book in The Tanach. Exodus is placed to have been written about 2047 BC plus or minus 12 years. To be off a century or two is understandable for ancient history, but to be off a millennium is a bit of a stretch. Also, Ramesses the Great, died in 1213 BC, yet the evidence as to Exodus has that book being written around 2200 BC.

"I know what you are thinking; enough with the dates already. But I wanted to give you information that shows these books were estimated to have been written by unknowns at vastly disparate time periods. After The Torah, the remaining 34 books are also in an order that has very little to do with when they were written. The Books have remained in that order since the Roman Catholic Athanasian Creed of 367 AD."

"The quotes, we will begin discussing tomorrow, will display the utter wrath of the God of The Tanach. By the scripture quotes, one can only believe that the God of The Tanach is full of vengeance, hate, contempt, and cruelty. Death seems to be God's justice. Unless this God of The Tanach is 'making nice' by only blinding people or not allowing the infirm to come to the alter. More of God's wrath in the form of raping, infanticide, rending the unborn from the bellies of their mothers, and forcing hundreds of thousands into slavery. But, we will get into all of that tomorrow. Don't forget group. Good night," said Zeus.

"Good bye," replied Grace. "Hurry back."

<<<>>>

"Grace. Grace," said Zeus

"Zeus. Zeus," replied Grace

"Oh, the songs and the poems and the prose are great for the congregation. So, you well know the scriptures are the most owned, and the least read. The second highest selling book in the United States is 'Atlas Shrugged' by Ayn Rand. That book is bought to be read unlike scriptures, which are bought to sit on the shelf. Less than ten percent of scripture owners ever read them. Now, what I want you to do is to sit up and take your Bible from your desk and open it to Genesis 2:16-17 and follow along. This will be the beginning of me pointing out to you the horror of The Tanach. I know your version will not exactly match the Ricci Version, but it will be close enough for you to get the point. Ready?" asked Zeus.

"Ready," replied Grace.

"Okay, Genesis 2:16-17. *'And the Lord God directing the man, said, Of all trees in the garden you are free to eat the fruit; however, as for the tree of knowledge of good and evil, you cannot eat from it, if you do you will surely die'.* You see, we have 'to die' in there."

"Now, onto Genesis 4:3-5,8. *'As time passed, Cain brought a gift to God from his harvest. And his brother Abel brought to God the best of his flock. The Lord was gratified by Abel's gift, but as for the offering from Cain God paid no attention. Cain was grief stricken and threw himself upon the ground ... and when they were out in the field Cain killed his brother Abel'.* Now, you have killing, but, oh, it gets worse."

"Go to Genesis 7:23. *'All existence on earth was no more, all living things on the earth and in the sky had perished. Only Noah, his wife and his sons and their wives survived'.* Everything is now dead except for eight people."

"Okay, go to Genesis 38:7. *'It was Er, Judah's son, his first born, was unsightly to God, and God killed him'*. Just killed him because God didn't like his looks."

"Exodus 12:29-30. *'It was at the midnight hour that God killed all the first born sons, and Egypt was without them. God killed the first born son of the Pharaoh. And God killed the sons of the lowly in the prisons. Each of the first born of all animals were killed. There was gnashing and wailing throughout Egypt. No home had been spared a death'*. And Jews celebrate this as Passover. What's to celebrate?" asked Zeus.

"I see your point," replied Grace.

"There is so much more. Let's really look into this," said Zeus.

"Just give me the chapter and verse," said Grace.

"Here goes," said Zeus. "Exodus 20:5. *'You will not salute or serve them. I am a God full of passion, and I bring guilt from the parents on to the children, into the third and fourth generations for those who turn against me'*."

"Exodus 21:15, *'If you strike your mother and father you will be killed'*."

"Exodus 22:18. *'They will die who lays down with an animal'*."

"Exodus 22:19. *'To God only will be brought sacrifices not to others or surely you will die'*."

"Exodus 23:23. *'You will follow my angel to the Hittites, Canaanites, Amorites, Jebusites, Perizzites, and Hivites and I will erase them from the earth'*. There are a lot of ...ites from The Tanach to the Book of Mormon."

"Exodus 31:12-15. *'And the Lord instructed Moses. The Sabbath day will be kept as a covenant forever for you and me. It makes you holy for the Sabbath day is a holy day. Any one not keeping it holy will die. If you work on that day you will surely be separated from the community. Six days of work and on the Sabbath rest. Those who choose not to rest will be wiped out'.* Grace, how many times did you work on the Sabbath?"

"Many," replied Grace.

"Exodus 32:26-29. *'Moses was in the camp and gave orders for those believing in the Lord to join him. The Levites walked towards him. The God of Israel has said that you are to arm yourself with your swords. You are to go into the camp and kill all the unbelievers. The Levites killed three thousand on the day. The Levites had obeyed, and Moses told them you are now ordained and will receive a great blessing'.*"

"Exodus 34:6-7. *'Hashem is slow to anger. God is gracious and is kind to the generations upon generations. He forgives sin, but he does not relieve all of their iniquity and puts punishment upon the third and fourth generations'.*"

"Who would want children if this was a fact? It's beyond reason," said Grace

"Leviticus 10:1. *'Nadab and Abihu, the sons of Aaron took a pan of fire with incense and placed it before Hashem that God had not asked for and they died'.*"

"Leviticus 20:9-10. *'If you curse your mother and father you will surely die. If a man sleeps with a married woman both she and the man will be put to death'.*"

"Leviticus 20:27. 'Fortunetellers will be killed, and they have no one to blame for their stoning'."

"Leviticus 21:16-23. 'God told Moses to talk to Aaron and tell him. If anyone through his generations has a defect they may not offer anything to God. Those of foul limb that is short or long, no one with a broken leg or arm, nor a midget or hunchback or who is blind or even has a growth in his eye, those who have had boils or suffered scurvy, can offer nothing before the Lord. He may not come before the alter or go behind the curtain for he has a defect. To do so is to profane the Lord'."

"You know, I have read all of this, and, well, just glazed over it, as I remember none of it. The very people who should have the grace of the, the Lord shunned," said Grace.

"Wrath, death, and destruction. It goes on," said Zeus.

"Leviticus 24:16. 'And one who blasphemes the name of the Lord will be put to death by being stoned by all of the community'."

"Leviticus 27:28-29. 'All the property anyone owns, beast, land, or man. Nothing that he has offered to the Lord will be given away or sold, nor can they be ransomed. The owner will be put to death'."

"Numbers 1:48-51. 'As God orders the Levites will be relieved from the census. The tabernacle is to be put under the responsibility of them. They must travel with the tabernacle. They will set it up no matter where they travel. Anyone, not a Levite, who approaches the tabernacle will be killed'."

"Numbers 25:1-9. 'At the encampment on the banks of Acacia the Israelites sleep with the women of the Moabite tribe. They also worshiped the idols *of the Moabites. The Israelites worshiped Baal and brought the Lord to anger. The Lord told Moses to gather the Israelites to his camp. Moses ordered that they will all be killed for their worship of Baal of Pero. A Midianite woman was brought into the camp by an Israelite. The Levite priest of the tabernacle saw this desecration. A man named Phinehas rushed the man and killed him with a spear thrust through his body and into the body of the woman, killing them both. The desecration brought a curse upon the Israelites and 24 thousand people died'."*

"So much killing, how could I have been blind to all of the needless killing?" said Grace.

"There are many more, that we will not cover, many, many more. Here are a couple more, though, to make my point," said Zeus. "Deuteronomy 13:1-5,7. *'There could be prophets among you who conjure the future and tell you they will give you signs, and they state the signs will take place along with miracles. If the prophets then tell you to worship the Gods of other nations, God says do no hear them. Your heart is being tested of your love of God. Fear the Lord alone. Do what the Lord prescribes and hear what he says. These false prophets must be put to death for they talk of flight away from the Lord. The same Lord that took you from slavery in Egypt. These prophets try to keep you from believing in the Lord you must kill them. If any one of your family should tell you to secretly worship other Gods, pity them, do not look upon them, but kill them. The remainder of the community will join you. Stone them, to death and never again allow such evil in your community'."*

"Deuteronomy 17:2-5. *'Suppose a man or woman has done a disgrace in the light of the Lord they have worshiped the sun and have broken the covenant with the Lord. Listen for it, and when you hear it take that man and woman to the gates and stone them to death'*. Again, another example of a 'benevolent' God," said Zeus."

"Deuteronomy 17:12. *'If a man should violate the renderings of a verdict of a priest they must be killed. Israel will not tolerate this conduct'*."

"Deuteronomy 18:20. *'Any prophet who claims to speak in my name that I did not so command or who speaks in the name of false gods must die'*."

"Deuteronomy 23:3. *'No bastard will enter the community of the Lord and onto the 10th generation will they not be allowed to enter'*."

"These verses are just in The Torah, the first five books. It would appear by these verses, God didn't care for his own creation, always seeking ways to punish humankind with death, sometimes a horrible death. But there is one more I must set before you that is so horrific, one would never believe it was from The Torah, but it is," said Zeus.

"Second Kings 2:23-24. *'The prophet Elisha went to Betel. As he walked young boys came out to laugh at him. They laughed at him because he was bald. Elisha turned to them and swore against them in the name of God. After Elisha's request from the Lord two she bears came from the woods and killed 42 of the children'*."

Grace's mind was racing. "They were just children. How horrible, I don't remember studying that in seminary," said Grace.

Zeus continued. "There are others you should look up, equally horrific. Of these horrid events, there are four in Joshua, four in Judges, two in First Samuel, one in Second Samuel, three in First Kings, three in Second Kings, one in Second Chronicles, one in Proverbs, three in Ezekiel, one in Isaiah, three in Jeremiah, and one in Zechariah. I have to give you two more short versions. Jephthah made a vow to the Lord that if the Lord gives him victory over the Ammonites, '*I will give the Lord the first thing coming out of my house to greet me when I return victorious. I will sacrifice that person to God as a burnt offering*'. Well. As luck would have it, the first person to come out of his house when he returned was his daughter. And the verse reads, '*her father kept his vow and she died a virgin*'."

"The Second is the story of Job. God asks Ha Satan if Satan would consider his servant, Job. God says Job is a blameless and upright man. To prove that Job is an upright and believing man, God makes a bet with Satan that no matter what Satan does, Job will remain loyal to him. Satan takes the bet and then set out to really mess with Job. Satan kills Job's servants, livestock, children, and wife. Then Satan burns Job's house to the ground then takes all of Job's wealth. And to add a further punishment Satan covers Job in boils. Through all of this Job is faithful to God, but the boils prove to be too much. Job pleads for mercy from God and then God gives Job back his family and wealth. All because of a bet!"

"Why would someone worship such a God as is portrayed in the verses I just spoke of? Simply put, they were terrified of such an inhumane, wrath filled God of their own imagination?"

"In 'The God Delusion', Richard Dawkins writes, 'The God of The Christian Old Testament is arguably the most unpleasant character in all fiction: jealous and proud of it; petty, unjust, unforgiving control-freak; a vindictive, bloodthirsty ethic cleanser; a misogynistic, homophobic, racist, infanticidal, genocidal, filicidal, pestilential, megalomaniacal, sadomasochistic, capriciously malevolent bully'."

"This is so much to absorb. How could I have read it and not questioned it before? You have certainly turned me off as to The Christian Old Testament," said Grace.

"Not to belabor my point, but I have two more quotes from the Apocrypha, that you should hear," said Zeus.

"I'm listening," replied Grace.

"The first is from First Esdras 1:51-53. 'His messengers were disturbed and of God's prophets, they were ridiculed. Their people had ungodliness and the king of the Chaldees came up against those prophets and within sight of the holy temple the young men, or maid, the elderly or the children were not spared the sword'. More false prophets. Now onto the second. 'The Wisdom of Solomon, 14:21-27. 'And the world was received for men served tyranny. They were wrong in their knowledge of God. They slew their children in sacrifices and met in secret. Their marriages were defiled, there was manslaughter, dissimulation, theft, corruption, tumults, perjury, souls were defiled, and uncleanliness. It was from the worshiping of idols. It was to be the end of all evil. The heathens were condemned to die'."

"I can't help myself. There is so much for you to know, to understand. These are things you have known, but, have ignored all of your adult life. These things can't be ignored, this time. On with the journey. The Books of the Apocrypha were written by anonymous scribes, and sages. Let me give you a little history," said Zeus. "The Apocrypha book Tobit was set in the 8th century BC, but its composition is dated as late as the 2nd century BC."

"The Book of Judith of the Apocrypha and the story of Susanna were set in the 6th century BC, but the compositions were dated in the 2nd century BC."

"Translating the Hebrew Bible into Greek is called the Septuagint meaning 70 for 70 scribes."

"The completion of the Masoretic or Jewish Bible dates to around the 10th century AD."

"Y H W H or Yahweh means 'He who causes to be'."

"The iniquities of the father are visited upon the children of the third and fourth generations. Exodus 34:6-7."

"In the Battle of Jericho God had Joshua's soldiers' parade around the city for seven days, thus ignoring the Sabbath."

"'The sun stood still, and the moon stopped'. Joshua 10:13."

"In the Septuagint First and Second Chronicles are called 'The things left out'."

The Book of Daniel, set in 600 BC, was not completed until 165 BC."

"The Talmud was not written until the 3rd century through the 5th century of AD."

"Jews in the 1st century AD in Palestine, including the supposed Jesus, spoke Aramaic."

"The dates of The Book of Joel range from the 9th century to the 5th century BC."

"Jonah was swallowed by a giant whale, but in Hebrew it is 'dag gadol' meaning big fish."

"The final forms of the Song of Songs were not written until 500 years after Solomon's reign."

"*'My God, my God, why have you forsaken me'* is in Psalms 22:1. Later to supposedly be repeated by Jesus on the cross."

"The angel Gabriel appears in The Tanach, The New Testament, and The Book of Mormon."

"Methuselah lived for 969 years, which, according to the time line of The Tanach, means he lived 14 years after the flood. And, he was not even on the ark. Go figure."

"I never heard of that last one," said Grace.

"Wait until we get to the mixed-up dates in The New Testament, which we will begin tomorrow night. Don't miss group. You are going to hear some things that are very interesting. Good night, Grace," said Zeus.

"Good bye, Zeus," replied Grace.

CHAPTER SEVEN

TWELVES AND THE VIRGIN BIRTHS

"Naomi, would you like to share?" asked Ginny.

"Well, I know that this is a secular institute. I mean we don't even have visiting clergy or services. But, since Grace arrived, it has given me a lot to think about … things spiritual … and all. I would like to talk about Ezra again. If that is alright?" asked Naomi.

"Certainly," replied Ginny.

"The third time Ezra had been in a church was when his half-brother was to be baptized," began Ginny. "His half-brother was but a few months old and Ezra's step-father wanted to have the ceremony. Ezra was nine and they had him baptized, also. Ezra didn't understand what it was all about; the water on the head and everything. Ezra had the feeling he was just dragged along for the ride. Also, it was the first time Ezra had seen his mother and step-father in church. The second time for Ezra was when he and his mother attended a wedding. But back to the baptism. Of course, Ezra, being only nine years old did not know that if he died before being baptized he would have had to spend eternity in limbo. Some have been there for 8 hundred years. Limbo is a place where those not baptized go. Then in 2007, there was a release from this limbo curse. The Pope ended the state of limbo for babies not baptized. So, after all that time, babies can now go to heaven."

"It seemed this decision by Benedict XVI was a result of a Vatican study. The study found it was alright for babies to go to heaven based on serious grounds. It seems in the 5th century, Saint Augustine concluded that unbaptized babies would go right to hell."

"Now, to put this in perspective, Ezra was not a Roman Catholic and the church where the baptism took place was not a Catholic church. So, would limbo have applied to Ezra? But all this limbo stuff is just that; stuff. Not even the Pope knows what happens after death. There is only 'belief' and 'faith' as to what happens to someone after they die."

"I looked up limbo after Ezra did and I talked about this. It was in the Encyclopedia Britannica, on-line of course. Well, it seems that according to Catholic theology, limbo is between heaven and hell where souls go who are not gifted to go to heaven nor are they condemned to hell. The concept of this whole, ridiculous, limbo thing was started in the middle ages as church dogma. It was just made up. Also, limbo is a place where the mentally impaired go. So, if someone is schizophrenic or bipolar they can't go ... well ... anywhere but limbo."

"Now, the question remains; what about all those unbaptized kids who have been in limbo for 8 hundred years? Also, now get this. Christian Old Testament saints were to be held in limbo until they were released by Jesus."

"Ezra and I are both bipolar, so, do we go to limbo. So, are we just 'Children of a Lesser God' as the movie goes? I have more to share, but for right now, I'll just shut-up."

"Do you want to share Grace, since your name came up?" asked Ginny.

"Yes, I think I will. I never really told my father how I felt about some of the things that went on in my early days in church. My father gave polite sermons. He didn't jump up and down like a wing-nut, so to say. Behind his pulpit was a huge cross with Christ on it. His message was about the same each week. He would tell the congregation about living in Christ and that sin would separate them from him. He told us all we had to accept Christ as our savior to go to heaven. I can't remember him ever saying what would happen if we did not accept Christ. I never heard him use the word hell."

"About Christ on the cross. Crucifixion was abolished during the reign of Constantine; a full 300 years plus, after the death of Christ. About that, it reads in First Peter 2:24, *'and he himself bore our sins in his body on the cross, so that we might die to sin and live to righteousness; for by his wounds you were healed'*."

"Supposedly, doing so, relieving the sin that is, means that Christ, the son of God influences and intervenes in the universe. But, as I investigate Deism, I realize that the First Cause does not do that. Thus, there is no threat of going to hell. It is unreasonable that there is such a place," said Grace.

"Okay, time's up. Doris and Becca, you will have plenty of time to share during the four o'clock group. That's it for now. Ginny ... Grace ... well done," said Ginny.

<<<>>>

"Grace. Grace."

"Zeus. Zeus."

"Good evening. We are going to deal with the 12s, and the lineage of mythology," said Zeus.

"12s?" asked Grace.

"You will see how many times the number 12 comes up. The sun moves south for six months but stops its movement south for three days. The sun, of course, does not move South. It is the Earth's rotation in relation to the sun. Never the less, the sun appears to stop moving on 22, 23, and 24 December. Then, on the 25 December, the sun starts to move north. The sun blocks out the Southern Cross and it is said 'the sun died on the cross' and was dead for three days; and, then, on 25 December was resurrected or born, again. Yet, this resurrection was not celebrated until the Spring Equinox, or the resurrection of Spring. Get the film 'Zeitgeist-The Movie' by Peter Joseph if you wish to learn more about this," said Zeus.

"I'll do that, but what about the number 12?" asked Grace.

"I am getting to that. It is important to point out the number 12. The 12 disciples are the 12 signs of the Zodiac which the sun or Jesus the Sun (Son) travels about with. The number 12 is replete throughout The Books of The Old and New Testaments as we will investigate." Zeus then listed the 12s of the scriptures.

"The 12 tribes of Israel."

"The 12 sons of Jacob."

"The 12 judges of Israel."

"The 12 great Patriarchs."

"The 12 Christian Old Testament prophets."

"The 12 kings of Israel."

"The 12 princes of Israel."

"The 12 apostles."

"The 12 disciples."

"The 12 supposed witnesses to the golden plates of The Book of Mormon."

"The 12 apostles of The Church of Latter Day Saints."

"Why so many 12s? A form of astrology was practiced in the First Dynasty of Mesopotamia from 1950 to 1651 BC. Even though we are all unique, astrology divides us up into 12s. Ever here 'what's your sign'? Those signs are the sun, the moon, the planets, a rising sun and the 12 houses. There are 12 signs in astrology and then there are the 12 'planets'; the sun, the North node of the moon, the South node of the moon, Mercury, Venus, Mars, Jupiter, Saturn, Uranus, Neptune, Pluto, and an asteroid called Chiron. You notice Earth is not mentioned as, even today, astrology is based upon the sun rotating around Earth. Go figure."

"Whoa, that is a lot of 12s. Nowhere in my studies did anyone point out the 12s in The Old and New Testaments. And, I certainly never picked-up on it myself. Please, continue," said Grace.

"The signs are divided into 12-month periods that denote your 'sign'. Of the 12 signs, six are male and six are female. The 12 signs are broken into four entities of three signs each, as to four elements; fire, earth, air, and water. The 12 signs are also broken into four seasons designated by a circle with a cross in the middle. So, those crosses you see on church steeples having a circle within the cross are denoting astrological signs of the four seasons," said Zeus."

"I always wondered why some churches had that type of cross on the steeple. We, most assuredly, did not study astrology in seminary," said Grace.

"Now to the lineage of the mythology of Jesus Christ. It all begins around 3000 BC. See if any of this sounds familiar."

"The first is Horus, around 3000 BC era, he was an Egyptian 'God'."

"Horus was born on 25 December. He was born of a virgin, there was a star in the east. He was adored by three kings. He was a teacher at the age of 12. He was baptized and began his ministry at the age of 30. He had 12 disciples. Horus performed miracles such as healing the sick and walking on water. He was referred to as the 'Lamb of God' and 'The Light'. He was betrayed and crucified. He was dead for three days and then was resurrected."

"Then there was the 'god' Dionysis, around 1500 BC to 1100 BC. Dionysis was a Greek 'god'. He, too, was born on 25 December of a virgin. He performed miracles such as turning water into wine. He was called 'King of Kings', 'Alpha and Omega', 'god's only begotten son. He died and was resurrected."

"Around 1400 BC, there was Mithra, a Persian. He, also, was born on 25 December of a virgin. He performed miracles. He was called 'The Truth and The Light'. He was dead for three days and then resurrected. Mithra was worshiped on Sundays."

"Attis is next; around 1200 BC. He, too, was born on 25 December of a virgin. He was crucified and was dead for three days before he was resurrected," said Zeus.

"All this makes my head spin. This alone makes me wonder about my religious beliefs even more so. Ah, but I still feel a spark," said Grace.

"Again, you will find this in the film 'Zeitgeist' about Jesus. Now, about Jesus. He had to be born before 4 BC, as Herod died in 4 BC. You know the story."

"Jesus was a Jew born on 25 December."

"Jesus was born of a virgin."

"There was a star in the East."

"Three Kings or Magi followed the star to locate and adorn the new savior. Ah, but, they arrived in Jerusalem two years after the birth of Jesus. More about that later."

"He was a child teacher at the age of 12."

"At 30 Jesus was baptized by John and thus began his ministry."

"He had 12 disciples."

"He performed miracles such as healing the sick, walking on water, and raising the dead."

He was called 'King of Kings, the son of God, Alpha and Omega, and the Lamb of God'."

"He was betrayed by his disciple Judas and sold for 30 pieces of silver."

"He was crucified, placed in a tomb, was dead for three days and then resurrected."

"Unbelievable! It's all a myth," said Grace.

"Oh, but there is more," said Zeus.

"If you go to your search engine and pull up 'livingstoneclass dot org' you can find this and more. In it there is a comparison of Joseph of The Christian Old Testament with Jesus Christ."

"Joseph, of the 'Coat of Many Colors' was hated by his brethren without a cause."

"Jesus says of himself 'they hated me without a cause'."

"Joseph was sold by his brothers."

"Jesus was sold by his brethren."

"Joseph was sold for 20 pieces of silver."

"Jesus was sold for 30 pieces of silver."

"Joseph was put into a pit which was meant to be a place of death for him."

"Jesus was crucified."

"Joseph was raised from the pit."

"Jesus was raised from the dead on the third day."

"They took council to kill Joseph."

"Pilate did not believe the accusation which was brought against the Lord Jesus. He found him innocent, yet he scourged Him."

"Joseph found favor in the sight of the jailer."

"In the case of Jesus, the Roman centurion said of Him, 'Truly this is the Son of God'."

"The birth of Joseph was miraculous in that it was by the intervention of God."

"Jesus was born of a virgin."

"It has all been there in writing, and I never made the comparisons," said Grace.

"Don't feel bad. Look at all the theologians who elect to ignore it. You may want to read 'god is not Great' by the arch atheist, Christopher Hitchens. In it he writes, 'When his mother, Mary, was espoused to Joseph, before they came together, she was found with child of the Holy Ghost'. 'Yes, and the Greek demi-god Perseus, was born when the god Jupiter visited the virgin Danae, as a shower of gold, and got her with child. The god Buddha was born through an opening in his mother's flank. Catlicus, the serpent-skirted, caught a ball of feathers from the sky and hid it in her bosom, and the Aztec god Huitzilopochtli was thus conceived. The virgin Nana took a pomegranate from the tree watered by the blood of the slain Agdestris, and laid it in her bosom, and gave birth to the god Attis. The virgin daughter of the Mongol king awoke one night and found herself bathed in a great light, which caused her to give birth to Genghis Khan. Krishna was born of the virgin Devaka. Horus was born of the virgin Isis. Mercury was born of the virgin Maia. Romulus was born of the virgin Rhea Sylvia. For some reason, many religions force themselves to think of the birth canal as a one-way street ...'."

"Birth canal. Good grief!" said Grace. "This is a lot to take in."

"One more thing, and I'll let it go for the night," said Zeus.

"Okay, one more thing," replied Grace.

"In the temple at Amun," Zeus began. "... at the site of Luxor in Egypt appears a series of scenes depicting the divine birth of the king, a pharaoh of the 18th dynasty around 1570 BC. Amenhotep or Amenophis III reigned during the 14th century BC. The Luxor nativity imagery represents a significant artifact demonstrating pre-Christian religious motifs being incorporated into Christianity. There is the annunciation, the conception, the birth, and the adoration as described in the first two chapters of the Gospel of Luke. The scenes were mythical in Egypt and have been copied in the Gospels. The virgin birth of the Egyptian Messiah, Horus, is depicted there."

"Qi, known as the 'Abandoned One' and later became the god Houji was miraculously conceived. His mother became pregnant with him after stepping in a footprint of the god Shangdi, a god that lasted from 1600 to 1046 BC."

"Laozi was conceived when his mother gazed upon a falling star. He was born while his mother was leaning against a plum tree. Remember the pomegranate tree? Laozi was born an old man with a grey beard. He was known as 'Old Master' or 'Old Child', around the 6th century BC."

"There is a legend of the late Yi, who was the Emperor Taizu of Liao. The legend is that the sun fell into the bosom of his mother and she became pregnant. When Yi was born, the room was filled by light and the smell of perfume. Yi was born with the body of a three-year-old and he began walking at the age of three months."

"If Christians knew about these gods, can you imagine the reactions? One can put it all together, that the story of Jesus Christ comes from a long line of mythology over a 3,000-year period. It is coincidental as to when the written word began around 3100 BC. So, the mythology of those gods was passed down to the mythology of Jesus Christ. All the other 'gods' ascended into heaven."

"Whoa," said Grace. "It's just so much to absorb."

"And it is what is. Am I starting to relieve your doubts about your doubts?" asked Zeus.

"How could it not?" replied Grace.

"Okay, time to go. Don't miss your appointment with Thelma. Night," said Zeus.

"Good bye and thanks," said Grace.

CHAPTER EIGHT

SO MANY QUESTIONS

Lorna, the orderly, knocked on Grace's door.

"Hi, Lorna, come on in," said Grace.

"Thelma sent me here to tell you that she had to cancel your eight o'clock," said Lorna.

"Why? What for?" asked Grace.

"Well … let's just say she has a situation … someone needs her attention right now," said Lorna.

"I hope it is not serious," said Grace.

"I hope not, too," said Lorna. "Thelma told me to tell you that you are getting stronger and missing one session will be okay."

"Getting stronger, huh? That's good to know. I can miss one appointment with Thelma … I guess I won't snap," laughed Grace.

"No snapping," replied Lorna. "Off to breakfast?"

"Yes, being free from eight to nine gives me some time on my rig … gotta look-up some things," said Grace.

"Good. Come on. I'll walk with you to the dining room," said Lorna.

"I'd like that," said Grace.

<<<>>>

"Come right in," Thelma said to Naomi. "And, if you have to miss group today, it will be fine. I heard you were given a clonazepam yesterday evening. Were you agitated? And Why?" Thelma got up to close the door.

"It's just when I went to group yesterday afternoon ... well ... again ... Grace was there. I used to watch her," said Naomi.

"And now?" asked Thelma.

"Well ... she shared that she no longer has the faith she once had. She said her faith was fading. Well ... mine has faded and it disturbs me. I mean if Grace Sharp loses her faith ... well ... it scares me. I am all confused," said Naomi.

"So, why don't you talk to me about it," said Thelma.

"Well ... it all started when I was a kid. I belonged to a Presbyterian church in a small town in the Midwest. Webster Groves. It is a town in Missouri near Saint Louis. Mother would take us to services ... my brother and me. We were told we were being good by going to church every Sunday. Our mother would drop us off, go home and then sleep as she worked the night shift at a hospital. Dad would either go home or go to work. I remember that the only time my dad ever went to church was on Christmas."

"I had a lot of questions. Why was I going to church with my brother and my parents didn't go? Was I a good person and are my parents bad people? What did church have to do with being good or bad? These were some of my questions when I was in grade school."

"When we moved to Tulsa, Oklahoma, mother said she wanted to start going to a different church. I later learned she was talking about changing religions. I didn't understand why dad wasn't happy about that or why he let mother know it. I remember them having some arguments about which church to go to. He wanted to go to a Methodist church. When I was older, I learned that he loved the Methodist hymns. But, at the time this was going on, still in my early teens, it didn't make any sense for them to argue where to go...I thought it was the same God, so what did it matter. Besides, they weren't regular church-goers," said Naomi.

"So, which church did you end up going to?" Thelma asked.

"You might say that dad won the first round, sort of. Mom told dad that if he went to church regularly with us, as a family, she would agree to go to a Presbyterian Church that was close to home, on Yale. To this day, I have no idea why they agreed on a Presbyterian Church let alone, that one. But, I do remember I didn't like it from the beginning because of the way it looked. It was so modern, so unlike any church I had ever seen. There was purple glass just about everywhere. When I really started to question my faith, I was curious if that purple church was still there, so I looked it up on the computer. It's still there and still looks as ugly as it did then."

"Looking back on it all, them arguing about which church to go to...it just wasn't worth the strife it created between them. I'm not sure how long we stayed at that church, but it wasn't that long. For a while, I remember that we did go as a family, it seemed just about every Sunday. I did like that and I did like the minister. Wish I could remember his name...but can still see him in my mind. After a couple of years, about the time I went into high school I think, dad stopped going with us. I have no idea why and it wasn't ever discussed in the family, that I can remember. He did go with us on Christmas and Easter, but that was about it," said Naomi.

"When this happened, when your dad stopped going, what did your mom do? Did you keep going to the same church?" Thelma was curious to know."

"It is interesting that you ask. To this day, I can't remember when mother had us start to go to the Episcopal Church. It just seemed to happen overnight that one day in church, I was wearing this lace scarf on my head and we did a lot of kneeling on the things attached to the pews. The minister, who was called a priest, wore lots of fancy robes and we genuflected every time we crossed in front of the cross on the altar. Without the robes, he wore the back-ward color that Catholic priests wear. At first, I had so many questions. Why did we have to, now, kneel? What difference did it make when we prayed whether we kneeled or not? Did that mean Presbyterians weren't going to go to heaven because they didn't? And it seemed phony in the beginning to genuflect. We had to bow when the cross was brought into the church, up the isle and when it was taken out of the church, when the service was over. Why? Why? Why? Just so many questions, especially since we had been raised as Presbyterians. I wondered why we used a missal for the service and not a Bible? Why did all the girls and women have to wear a head covering when in the sanctuary? Why couldn't we go beyond the kneeling rail when communion was served?

What did the priests mean when they said it was the 'real' blood and the 'real' body of Christ after the priests blessed the wine and the wafer? What did it mean by telling me I could not take communion until I was a member and then a full-fledged Episcopalian? I had been taking communion at the Presbyterian church. Why the confirmation classes to become a member? A member of what? And, what was being confirmed?"

But, since my brother and I had been raised in our family, where children were to be seen and not heard, I knew better than to ask mother why we had even changed to become Episcopalians. I just knew it was important to her. In time, I began to feel like I fit in and I learned to like the traditions of the church, even though most I never really knew why we did many of them. I guess we were brain-washed, you might say. My brother became an altar boy, I did my catechism classes in order to become a member of the church and was really involved in the youth church activities. I even went to a couple of summer camps that were for Episcopalian high school kids. Religion was really a big deal for me at this point in my life. I remember even giving a sermon from the pulpit. Seniors graduating from high school were asked to give a sermon that they wrote. It was a very big deal and I felt really proud that I was able to do this. I wore my cap and gown when I gave the sermon," said Naomi.

Thelma listened to every word. It gave her a really good idea of her background. She couldn't help but ask, "What was it like once you went off to college? Did things change for you?"

"Don't know what happened or why, but while I was away at college, I lost my faith, more and more, year by year. Funny, too, as I was losing my faith and interest in the church, dad started going to church with mom. He even went back to school to get an accounting degree. At the time, I couldn't really accept the fact that he had gone back to school and seemed to become a holier than thou person. I felt he was too old to go back to school ...that it wasn't fair that he was going to school. It seemed like he was taking money from us, especially me, so that I had a hard time at college because I barely had enough to make ends meet each month even with a scholarship. On top of it, with my faith diminishing with each year of college I found fault with him 'finding God'.' It seemed hypocritical. He sure hadn't been like that when we were growing up," said Naomi.

"Did this change your relationship with your dad?" asked Thelma.

"It certainly didn't help. No, it would be a rocky road...me, dad, and religion...even up to when he died. But, when I fell madly in love in my sophomore year in college. I knew I wanted to be married in the Episcopal church. My family was excited for me and fences seemed to mend, but only for a while. My fiancé and I made a trip back to Tulsa for the weekend that I had set-up an appointment for us to talk about wedding plans with Father Wilcox. I so loved this priest and was eager for his approval. Well, within one sentence of meeting with Father Wilcox, I felt the church had betrayed me...that Father Wilcox was the enemy and that the God that I loved was now keeping me from what I wanted so bad, to be married in the Episcopal Church," said Naomi.

"My gosh, Naomi, what happened in that meeting?" Thelma could barely get out her question, feeling Naomi's anger even after all these years.

"Father Wilcox," began Naomi. "Explained to us that before we could be married, we would have to get permission from the bishop. What! Get permission to get married? From the bishop? Why? I hadn't been told any of this when I was growing up in the church and learning it this way, supposedly the happiest time in my life, I was so upset. I had been a good Episcopalian member. But, it turned out that since my fiancé had been married before and was now divorced, we had to have the bishop's permission. Plus, we had to go to these special pre-nuptial classes that lasted six months. And, it would be better, too, for the marriage if he would become a member of the church. I was dumbfounded with all that Father Wilcox explained that we needed to do before we got married. I wasn't rude to Father Wilcox when we left, but I knew I wouldn't be back...not to this church. We were married in a Methodist church, but this incident only made me ask more about my faith"

"Who was responsible for that man-made rule as to who could and who couldn't get married in an Episcopal church, but it was alright in the Methodist church? They were both Christian ... it made no sense to me. Another incident, not too long after I was married, my best friend from church got married. We met for lunch before the wedding. She told me she was having to get married...she was 4 months pregnant. She didn't show, yet, though. When I went to the service at the same Episcopal church we had grown-up in, that I had so wanted to be married in, it was hard to sit through the service and be happy for her. How was it alright for her to get married in the church, in a white dress...and be pregnant? There weren't any good answers. In the church, she had 'sinned', but since no one in the church knew she was pregnant, except for a handful of close friends and family, she had the wedding I felt I also deserved. But, no, there were the man-made rules. After that happened, the only time I went to that church is when I went home, and my parents were going. Maybe Christmas, Easter and Mother's Day. But I never took communion when I went."

"The next time I had to ask myself about my belief in God was when a special person in my life was dying. What happens to a person when they die, and they aren't a Christian? That question is probably my biggest question about religions...that I never did get a good answer or let's say, the answer I had hoped for. I became a surrogate daughter and they, surrogate parents. And they were Jewish. But, that didn't matter to me. From our first meeting, we just became 'family'. We shared a life together for almost ten years. However, when the lady who had been like a mother-sister-friend for so long became extremely ill, I was concerned about what was going to happen to her soul when she died. I did not know about a Jewish afterlife but remembered hearing that when a Jewish person died, since they didn't believe in heaven or hell, well...nothing happened after they died. They just lived, and then, just died. Even though I hadn't been a member of church for years, now that she was within days of dying, I was concerned as to what was going to happen to her after she died. I had been raised that unless you believed in Jesus Christ and asked him to forgive you of your sins, you couldn't go to heaven. I still very much believed in this about heaven and

82

hell. But, I also really began to question the concept of 'hell' and 'heaven' knowing how kind and supportive both of these Jewish people had been to me, treating me like a daughter they had lost from suicide. They loved me, and I loved them, as special as any family member by blood. I made an appointment with the minister of the Methodist church, who I knew. I didn't feel comfortable talking to my parents about this, especially not my dad. When I explained to her my concern, she pointed to all of these books piled high in the corner of her room. She said that all of them talked about heaven, about the love of God, about Jesus Christ dying on the cross for our sins so that we could go to heaven, and on and on. You get the picture. I listened and began to hear her telling me that because my dear friends were Jewish and didn't believe in Jesus Christ, they weren't going to go to heaven when they died. I didn't direct my angry feelings toward this minister who had just told me that these two people were going to hell when they died. I thanked her the best I could and left without asking her any more questions. It was pretty obvious to me, she believed what she had just told me. As for me, I was every bit as mad as I had been when I was told I couldn't be married in the Episcopal Church. I could not, and I would not believe that these people were going to go to hell. He had been Social Security Administrator under Eisenhower, been President of Brandis University, had helped the Jews that had been in the Nazi war camps find relatives to live with once freed from those horrific camps. She had been by his side for more than sixty years, a devoted loving wife. No, you couldn't tell me that God would have them spend eternity in hell. That was not the God I prayed to and felt I knew."

"I went to Arlington with her husband to bury her. At the grave site, I said a prayer to God, to please take care of her as I knew He would, being the God I felt I knew. But, my faith in any religion was shattered. At this point, I hadn't totally given up on God. I just wasn't a believer of any faith, anymore, for almost 40 years."

"Something happened to change this?" asked Thelma.

"Yes, and it totally caught me off guard. It was shortly after my second husband passed away. The hospice that had taken care of him held a service in a well-known Episcopal Church for all of those that had died in the last six months. Still very distraught at the loss of my husband and feeling very, very alone I attended this service with my mother. Being back in the Episcopal environment, sitting in the pews, kneeling, genuflecting, all the things I had questioned and then scorned...well ... while the service was taking place, I felt I was being 'called' to return to the church. After that service, I started going to this church every Sunday. It didn't take me that long to be became involved in the church activities, also. I eventually decided to join. When the bishop visited the church, I was 'allowed' to become a member, having gone through some refresher courses. I became very involved and felt comfortable, at first, feeling I was 'back home' and it felt good."

"I became a member of the alter guild and the building fund committee. I also became involved in the event committee and helped the office do some upgrades on their computer. However, as I got to know people in the church better and saw their interaction with each other and the priests, it became evident that what seemed to be a placid, godly place on the surface was in fact a back-stabbing, cliquish, do it my way or else environment. It was worse than what takes place in a work environment where things are not done 'in the name of God'. There were two factions of membership where one faction ruled and the other wanted to rule. They bickered back and forth, talked badly about each other, and those on the building fund committee took advantage of their positions, taking financial gain from the church on contracts, for work they did for the church. Disgusted was not the word for it. I was appalled at the way the deacons and other heads of the church bad-mouthed the priest. What I had felt about the church when I was younger was made even worse with all that I saw happening in this church."

"The last straw was how they handled the three Christmas Eve services. It was a small church, and to give the regular church-goers an assured seat for one of these services, the church gave out 'tickets' to get in. If you had a ticket that night, you could get right in. If you didn't, you had to wait to see if there were any empty seats after those with tickets had been seated. Those empty seats were filled with first come, first seated. The second Christmas I was there, an acquaintance asked me if I could get tickets for three...it was for her, her husband, and his mother, who was the widow of an Episcopalian priest. She was visiting from California. With my position in the church by now, it was easy to get the tickets. But, the more I thought about what I had done and why, I wasn't at all pleased with myself let alone the church. That night, I was an usher. When I seated them, and they thanked me, I knew my church-going days were numbered. When I tried to talk to the priest about this, it was a lost cause. Not because of his belief or not in God. No, it was apparent to me that he, too, was now more wrapped-up in the day-to-day operations of the church than tending to his flock."

"Why is there so much hypocrisy when it comes to religion? Is it a thought process, that if one attends church they are more destined to go to heaven than one who abstains from attending church? When my husband came into my life via a computer dating service at the end of 2007, I left the Episcopal church and even though my husband was a secular Jew, we started to go to a 'modern' church. Attending that church did not feel comfortable for me because it lacked what I would call 'tradition'. Instead of a missal, the services were all Bible related and a lot of singing, singing, and singing. I lost interest soon after we started attending. We stayed with it for a while, had the minister marry us outside of the church, and then we really lost interest and stopped attending."

"After my husband and I first started dating, he introduced me to a book 'Conversations with God'. I couldn't put it down. As I read 'the book' it seemed to 'say' things in a way that I felt and believed what God was really like. I do recall, as I read it, ... well ... I wondered if the author really had conversations with God. But, I did feel, regardless, that the author had the best concept, so far, about who God was and what God was all about. My husband even got a workbook that went along with Conversations with God. We spent our evenings going over the workbook, together."

"My husband discovered that the author was having a workshop in Oregon. The seminar was a review of his teachings. Well ... it turned out to be sort of a let-down and I was not impressed. The author was the leader of the entire seminar. By the time of this workshop, the author had remarried, and the workshop was more about his new wife than his work. She was a poet and read her writings at the seminar. After returning home, although impressed with the lessons in the book, I felt pretty sure the author never had a 'conversation with God'."

"There was another incident that left its mark on my heart. I'm rambling on. I guess you have heard enough. I've already missed morning group," said Naomi.

"No, no, please go on I am very interested," replied Thelma.

"Okay, then. The mark on my heart relates to religion and given the circumstances I was dumbfounded. And this is why. A young man that worked for me when I owned an airport was but sixteen when he started. We were from different cultures, different socio-economic backgrounds ... well ... we educated each other. From the beginning, I took every occasion to close the gap between the young man and me. It was a gap that he so profoundly felt, and often was unable to hide. In time, with trust and patience, he became like a son I never had. I was to become the 'liberated' mother he did not have. We shared much, but we stayed mostly to our own cultures, but the 'love' between us has endured to this day."

"When his mother passed away, he, of course, asked me to attend all the services associated with burying her. At the mortuary, the church, and then, I went to the gravesite service. It was held in a separate cemetery, where the other Catholics were buried. The services in the mortuary were held in

Spanish. I respectfully followed what the others did as to standing, and kneeling, whatever was required. He wanted to have me sit up front with him, with his family. I did so at the mortuary, but at the church and gravesite, I stayed to the back."

"At the church, although most of the service was spoken in Spanish, when the priest had occasion to give instruction to the congregation, he spoke in English. The service was conducted very much like an Episcopalian service, but it was Roman Catholic. But, it was relatively easy for me to follow. When it came time for communion … well … get this, I knew I wouldn't take communion as the rules of their church were very much as with the Episcopalian rules, that unless you were a 'member', you couldn't participate. But I had anticipated that I would go forward to the alter, for my 'son', at least to be blessed. But, to my amazement, that was not to be the case. In a defiant, angry tone, the priest informed the congregation that unless you were a practicing Catholic, 'there was no point in coming to the alter to be blessed', let alone take communion. I was not recognized in that church as being a member of God's flock? I couldn't believe what I just heard. There, in a church, was a man of the cloth, who is supposedly to love and cherish all people of God, sinners especially, and he wasn't even going to bless us. I could hardly hold my anger. Another man making man-made rules about God."

"What was worse, my 'surrogate son' realized what had taken place, felt very bad about it to the point of feeling he needed to apologize for the priest's words ... on of all days, the day his mother was buried. It was a very sad moment, again all of this trouble 'in the name of God'," said Naomi.

"Whew, what a story. It seems clergy did everything they could to chase you the other way from religion," said Thelma.

"It seemed so. And not just the clergy. Members who called themselves Christians also had a lot to do with my present faith ... or lack of faith," said Naomi.

"Who have you told about these experiences?" asked Thelma.

"You are the first. I know Grace Sharp is having trouble with her faith, but I'm not. I have no faith. And, it took me a long time to get here. My mother and especially my dad were upset with me for leaving the church. Dad attributed it to me being bipolar. Ever since I was diagnosed ... well ... I have been a second- class citizen in my dad's eyes. I embarrass them. Dad is afraid someone will find out. If that happened the roof would cave in, or at least he thought so. Both my parents are gone. And, it would really be awful if someone knew I was in here. OMG!" laughed Naomi.

"We have your meds adjusted and you seem to be doing okay," said Thelma.

"All I need is a nurse practitioner. Someone to handle the meds. I don't need a couch," said Naomi.

"I am sure we can find you a nurse practitioner in Boston. I'll get on the computer ... I'll find one ... and I can probably give you a name this evening. I will, of course call and talk to them and decide who would be the best for you. Do you agree with that?" asked Thelma.

"You'll do all of that," said Naomi.

"Yes, I will get right on it. I think we are finished for now. I would like to see you tomorrow after the four o'clock group. After group is finished, come right to my office. We can talk before you go to dinner," said Thelma.

"I'll be here," replied Naomi.

"Good session today. Do you feel better?" asked Thelma.

"A lot better and I know my meds are kicking in," replied Naomi.

"See you tomorrow," said Thelma.

"Bye," replied Naomi.

CHAPTER NINE

INDULGENCES

"Zeus. Zeus."

"You know I am here. Yo, girlfriend," said Zeus.

"Yo, girlfriend. On what street corner do you hang out?" laughed Grace.

"Are you ready for a little Catholicism?" asked Zeus.

"I am ready," replied Grace.

"There are those that are impressed with the Roman Catholic brilliance," said Zeus.

"Roman Catholic brilliance," Grace interrupted. "It just dawned on me what it is we are really about. At first, I thought it was to assuage my lack of faith and the thought that I may have lost it all. You were allowing me to feel alright with myself. I still have guilt, but is it not about the guilt trip I am on, it is about the fact that this is all … should I say … made up by men. Ruth was probably written by a man," said Grace.

"Ruth was written by a man … trust me," replied Zeus. "And you are right on both counts," said Zeus.

"How is that?" replied Grace.

"I am trying to assuage your dilemma ... the guilt trip. But, I am also trying to show you that all scriptures are written by man. And these men had an agenda when they wrote them," said Zeus.

"Sorry I interrupted. Please continue," said Grace.

"Ah ... with Roman Catholic brilliance of its cardinals, archbishops, and bishops," began Zeus. "They are able to discern, that when someone dies, that person will go directly to heaven, take a short stay in purgatory, go to limbo, or go directly to hell. No one on the face of this Earth knows what happens to a person when they die. And, before you ask, nor do I. No one knows, except that is the cardinals, the archbishops, and the bishops. It is to their benefit if they know someone has gone to purgatory. Because they can sell indulgences."

"Indulgences?" asked Grace. "I know. Follow along."

"Purgatory, in the Roman Catholic doctrine is a place, a state of suffering, inhabited by the souls of sinners who are expiating their sins before going to heaven."

"To get out of purgatory a little sooner, one's family could pay the cardinals, the archbishops, and the bishops to decrease the time of a loved one in purgatory. Of course, the more souls in purgatory, the more geld or lira or pounds would cross the palms of the highest-ranking clergy of the Holy Roman church."

"In medieval times, the church used to sell 'indulgences' for money. This amounted for paying for some number of days' remission from purgatory, and the church literally, with breathtaking presumption, issued signed certificates specifying the number of days off that had been purchased. The Roman Catholic Church is an institution for whose gains the phrase 'ill-gotten' might have been specifically invented."

"Richard Dawkins in his book 'The God Delusion' wrote, 'And all of its money-making rip-offs, the selling of indulgences must surely rank among the greatest con tricks in history, the medieval equivalent of a Nigerian Internet scam, but far more successful',"

"As recently as 1903, Pope Pius X was still able to attribute the number of days' remission from purgatory that each rank in the hierarchy was entitled to grant; cardinals two hundred days, archbishops a hundred days, and bishops a mere fifty days. If you were rich, you could lay down a provision for your soul or someone else's soul in perpetuity."

"What amazes me is that the indulgences are counted in days. How do the cardinals, archbishops, or bishops know anything about the time line in purgatory? What is a day in purgatory? And, how is it decided that the soul is immortal?"

"I find this ongoing rip-off unbelievable. It must take the same thought processes as someone believing in the Roswell, New Mexico aliens. Those 'Greys' that crash landed there in 1947."

"Some believe it ... but ... belief is faith without proof," said Grace

"Ah, good old faith and belief. But, I find it no more foolish than cardinals selling indulgences to shorten someone's time in purgatory for two hundred days."

"'He loves you, and he needs money! He always needs money! He's all-powerful, all-perfect, all-knowing, and all-wise. But, he just can't handle money. Religion takes in billions of dollars, they pay no taxes, and they always need a little more.'"

"That's from a George Carlin routine. I've seen it on the internet," said Grace.

"**Right on. America's greatest philosopher, George Carlin,**" said Zeus.

"And, as a former televangelist, I must admit I am very guilty of that," said Grace.

"**You raked in millions, right?**" asked Zeus.

"Yes, I did, and it was not right," replied Grace.

"**You will figure out what to do with the money,**" said Zeus. "**So, let's continue. Did you ever notice how splendid the church is and the other buildings on the property, but there is always a 'building fund' or an African charity to provide water, medical care and a school. And when the minister and his wife visit it during the summer, they always stop for a week or two in Europe. Who pays for that? You get the point,**" said Zeus.

"**A well-known minister, who was also the president of a university was counseling a couple that were in a dire condition financially. The minister looked over the budget and exclaimed that he knew what the problem was. It seems the couple was not giving 10% to the church. Oh, I am sure that was a big help to their tight budget. That same minister blamed 9/11 on the LGBTQ community.**"

"On 'Last Week Tonight', John Oliver exposed televangelists. Those evangelical preachers, whose sole purpose is to get on television, and ask for funds for their ministries. I know you know all about this. They prey on the sick, poor, and desperate in order to line their pockets, and then they use that money to fund a lavish lifestyle that includes mansions, luxury cars, vacations, and more," said Zeus.

"That I never did," said Grace.

"I know that, and you should feel good about it," replied Zeus. "Toward the end of the segment, which quickly went viral, Oliver revealed that he had incorporated his own church, without any restrictions. He called it 'Our Lady of Perpetual Exemption'. The church worships the deity of the powerful and the lenient IRS. Oliver said he would begin accepting 'seed money' to build his new church, which would help him to cure people's ailments."

"It seems like a comedic bit; perhaps the most terrifying thing should be how little John Oliver had to act for the sketch. He merely repeated things the real televangelists have actually said."

"To quote Jennifer C. Martin from her book 'Making Money Off Miracles: The Gospel of Televangelists. 'Those televangelists follow the model of 'prosperity gospel' in which they believe that wealth is a sign of God's favor, and that by simply believing and praying for money – in addition to donating copious amounts of money to various Christian ministries – is what will take you there. Not surprisingly, most of the victims of this harmful prosperity doctrine are those in the poor and working class – it's like a monstrous pyramid scam of religions. They see prosperity theology as a supernatural lottery, which isn't shocking, considering that 61% of people who play the lottery are from the poorest one-fifth of the population. But these televangelists' claim that your faith, your very soul, is tied to giving 'positive confessions'. And the fact that you are poor isn't just bad luck: it is not having enough faith, not praying enough, and, of course, not giving a big enough donation to their ministry."

"She continues," said Zeus. "'The greed of scheming televangelists is just another symptom of a predatory line of thinking among the rich and powerful driven to further atrociousness by attaching the name of God to their actions'."

"Tithe or ma'aser dekate, meaning 10% comes from the Tanach whereby supposedly Abraham, when given a fortune in property, decided to return 10% to Malich Chazadec, the king of Jerusalem. There is the Christian question of, does one tithe the 10% before or after taxes? You can guess how that question is answered? Of course, they want it out of gross, not net. Deism requires no tithe."

"Ah, Deism again," said Grace.

"I think that is enough for now. Sweet dreams. Night," said Zeus.

"Bye," replied Grace.

<<<>>>

"Zeus. Zeus."

"Grace. Grace."

"Ah. I knew you were there," said Grace.

"S'up girlfriend," said Zeus.

"S'up girlfriend. You're hanging out on that street corner, again," said Grace.

"Down in the 'hood," laughed Zeus. "I have some real good stuff for you today."

"Stuff from the 'hood. Okay ... let's get started," said Grace.

"To begin with, let's discuss the 'versions' of the Bible," began Zeus. "All of The New Testament versions. Let's start with the 'Vulgate' or rather Vulgates. This is a Latin version from Aramaic or Hebrew or Greek, beginning with the 4th century. The Roman Catholics kept the Bible written in Latin until the 16th century. Protestantism ... started with the Lutheran movement, of course. Martin Luther first copied the Latin version into German. But, let's start with the first chapters of The New Testament. The gospels."

"Matthew, Mark, Luke, and John were all written after the death of their Messiah, Jesus Christ. The Bede Vulgate around 375 AD. By the way, from here on out tonight, for tonight, all dates will be AD. Anyway ... The Bede Vulgate was where the Gospel of John was lost. The King Alfred Vulgate included The Torah, the Ten Commandments, and possibly Psalms around 900. The Wessex Gospel contained the four Gospels around 990. The Ormulum Vulgate contained some passages of the Gospels and the Acts of the Apostles around 1150. We could go on and on, but suffice it to say, there are at least 14 Vulgate versions. I wanted to give you an idea as to when those versions were written. In The New

Testament, the gospels of Matthew, Mark, Luke, and John were written a full generation after the birth of Christ, or so the myth goes. The Books of The Tanach and The New Testament were formed, put together, edited, or however one wishes to state it, by the time of the Athanasian Creed being developed. But, none of the Vulgates date back as far as the Athanasian Creed, around 367. The Creed's first tenet is 'Whoever will be saved, before all things it is necessary that he hold the Catholic faith'. If you are not Catholic, you are unable to be saved. This is a belief that goes on to this day."

"The list you will find from on-line sources alone counts 15 Tanachs, and 127 New Testament versions. This is just a listing of a small example of the hundreds of versions; perhaps thousands. I have no idea. Just of the King James Version alone, there are five versions. The King James Bible, written in 1611, and The King James II Version was written in 1971, known as KJ2. The New King James Version was written in 1982, and The American King James Version was written in 1999. And to top off the five, The Divine Name King James Version of the Bible was written in 2011. Just from a rudimentary analysis, it can be surmised that much was interpreted and re-interpreted from the 4th century beginnings of the Vulgate version to the 2011 Divine Name King James Version. Also, the interpretations were not that easily determined, as Hebrew of the 4th century had no vowels. It was not until around 600 that vowels were beginning to be added. So, the interpretations up until then were not necessarily true to the Hebrew."

"Sometime, beginning around 600, a group of scribes in Tiberias called Masoretes, mesora meaning tradition, began developing a system of vowel marks, called neqqudot, to indicate how the text was traditionally read."

"So, did the versions around the time of the Athanasian Creed come from old Hebrew interpretations of the Vulgates or did they use the Greek interpretation to decide what written word would be placed in the Bible? The Books of the Bible were translated from Aramaic, to Hebrew, to Greek to Latin or from Hebrew directly to Latin. This leads one to believe that the early Vulgates were different from the Vulgates after the 7th century. Thus, adding even more versions to the Bible. A good example of how translations change is the 'helpmeet' dilemma from The King James Version to The New King James Version."

"The word *'helpmeet'* comes from Genesis 2:18 of The King James version of the Bible, *'It is not good that man should be alone, I will make a helpmeet for him'*. Meet in this context is an adjective that means 'suitable'. What is written is that God created a 'help' for Adam, as his helper did 'meet' a certain standard as in fit or proper. Through the years, the phrase 'help meet' morphed into a single word, 'helpmeet', which is sometimes used as a synonym for helpmate, meaning spouse or companion. Modern translations render the phrase 'help meet' to *'a helper fit for him'*, from The English Standard Version or a *'helper suitable for him'* from both The New International Version and The New American Standard Bible. And, in The New King James Version, it reads *'a helper comparable to him'*. You can read more on this at gotquestions dot org."

"There is a big difference between the versions. The New King James Version, which reads *'a helper comparable to him'* is the closest to The

Tanach. Printing of Bibles began around 1450 with the Gutenberg Vulgate Version. Thus, King James had the printed word to rely upon for his 1611 version of the Bible. And, it all could have been a simple type-o from 'mate' to 'meet'. The typesetter could just as well have made a mistake."

"I never thought of it that way … a type-o," said Grace.

"Well, it could have happened, going from German to English," said Zeus.

"But, if we look into The Stone Edition of The Tanach, again Genesis 2:18 it reads *'Hashem God said, 'It is not good that man be alone; I shall make a helper corresponding to him'.'*"

"Through millennia, from the spoken to the written word, the myth changed. The scriptures were not written by a God, they were written by man from the Vulgates to The New Divine Version of the King James Bible."

"Okay, that is enough for this session, don't you think?" asked Zeus.

"Yes, I have to get up and eat breakfast. I have an appointment with Thelma before group" said Grace.

"Do you like group?" asked Zeus.

"Yes … yes, I do, it is … well … fun," replied Grace.

"Good night," said Zeus.

"Bye for now," replied Grace.

CHAPTER TEN

IN THE THIRD PERSON

"Gracie."

"Oh, I hate that. Makes me sound like Gracie Allen, George Burns wife. He used to say, 'Say Goodnight Gracie' and she would reply 'Goodnight, Gracie'. Just silly. So, what do we have tonight? More 'versions'?" asked Grace.

"No more 'versions'," replied Zeus. "What we are starting out with is where did Jesus come from?"

"This ought to be good. I am ready," said Grace.

"Good, let's get started," said Zeus. "Of the 27 books of the Protestant New Testament, 52% are written in the third person. But, before we get into that, let's look into who decided that Jesus was the Messiah and the son of God."

"Though Jesus is thought of as the Messiah, it was not until 325 AD that the Nicene Creed decided for all of Christianity that Jesus was in fact God and was part of the trinity of God, the holy spirit, and Jesus being the Son of God. Not monotheistic, but three Gods. Flavius Constantine, the Caesar of the Roman Empire, called together three hundred or more bishops and leaned on them to decide about Jesus. In effect, to settle the matter of who Jesus was. And they argued about Jesus being the Son of God."

"The Council of Nicea voted to make the full deity of Jesus the accepted position of the church."

"Get this, they voted on it. This meant that some of the bishops were preaching the divinity of Jesus; yet, not truly believing in their doctrine. It had to come to a vote. Suppose it had gone the other way? The entire New Testament would have become worthless."

"Constantine adopted the Catholic faith and I imagine the three hundred plus bishops called to the Council of Nicea were Catholic. Who else would he have called to the council? There were fringe Christian sects. It makes one wonder how they felt about Jesus before they came to the council and what their vote was. In essence Jesus Christ was voted into divinity. He was and the 'Good Book' was saved. So, let's venture into the 'Good Book'."

"Mathew, Mark, Luke, and John ... the four Gospels were written after Jesus Christ was crucified, died, resurrected, and ascended into heaven as the myth goes. Scholars present the dates of the writing of the Gospels that do not jibe. The dates range from 65 through 95 AD. And, 68 through 110 AD. If the 68 through 100 AD dates are true, it would mean that the Gospel of John could have been written after The Book of Revelation, which we shall address in due time."

"Dates also present another dilemma and that is the writings of the Apostle Paul which are listed to have been written before the Gospels of Matthew, Mark, Luke, and John from 51 to 70 AD. But it is agreed that the Gospels and Paul's letters were written after the death of Jesus. So, there were no eye witness accounts; and, thus they were written in the third person."

"The New Testament Gospels were written between 65 and 95 AD, though scholars have no way of knowing exactly who 'The Book's' authors were. Plus, in ancient times many other Gospels existed, perhaps as many as 30."

"All but the four Gospels were lost or eliminated as they were considered 'heretical texts. By lost I mean burned or otherwise destroyed as in the 4th century, at the behest of the teachings of the now Saint Irenaeus, a second century bishop of Lyon in Gaul of the Roman Empire."

"There was a 5th Gospel. The Gospel of Thomas, but it was rejected as a forgery as it was supposedly written long after Thomas was dead. Plus, the Gospel of Thomas promoted Gnosticism, a second century heretical doctrine."

"The point is that it is established that these books were not divinely inspired. They were written by men who held councils as to which of the 'divinely inspired' books should be in the Bible and they, mere men, trashed the other books. And, it was the bishops that, who gave their permission to marry, and remit 50 days off of purgatory. They were the same bishops that destroyed 20 plus Gospels."

"I guess the bishops didn't notice that the time line was off as to the four Gospels and the epistles of Paul. As Paul came onto the scene after Matthew, Mark, Luke, and John. And, even the time-line for John was way off as scholars have him writing the Gospel as late as 110 AD, yet he supposedly wrote The Book of Revelation in 94 AD. The epistles of John are dated from 90 to 110 AD. Was John of the Gospels, John of Revelation, and John the writer of the epistles, the same John? So, are we to assume that John was a megalomaniac writing in the third person in the Gospel, yet he got his first person act together for the epistles and Revelation?"

"No one. No professor ever taught that in seminary. You are starting to open my eyes," said Grace.

"I hope so. We have a long way to go before they are fully open. Well, I have given you enough to think about this morning. Go eat, see Thelma, and enjoy your group. I will see you tonight. Bye," said Zeus.

"Bye," replied Grace.

"The New Testament is to be the 'loving' teaching of Jesus."

"Boy, you are getting right to it, aren't you?" said Grace.

"Yeah, it's going to be a short night. I want to wrap up The New Testament," said Zeus. "All but the last book. You'll see."

"Okay, let's get this short night started," said Grace.

"As I said, the 'loving' teachings of Jesus. Let's start off with. Luke 2:14," said Zeus.

"You saying the chapters as one, two, three ... well ... you sound like Trump the time he said 'two Chronicles' instead of 'Second Chronicles'. What a yutz," said Grace.

"I just do it for brevity," said Zeus.

"Oh, that didn't sound right. You are not a yutz," said Grace.

"You are so funny. Anyway ... go to Luke 2:14, it reads '... *and on the Earth, peace and good will toward humankind'*," said Zeus. "And then go to Luke 19:27, in the morning of course, not now. The verse is written '*Jesus said, but these enemies of mine who do not want me to reign over them, bring them here and slay them in my presence'*, in a Parable. So much for peace on Earth."

"In Luke 22:36 it is written, '*Then Jesus said unto them ... he without a sword, sell his garment and buy one'.*"

"Listen to this story," said Zeus. "In Acts 5:1-11. '*There was a man named Ananias, who with Sapphira his wife, sold property. Ananias brought some of the money but not all of it to the apostles. Ananias claimed it was all of the money. His wife agreed with keeping some of the money back. Peter said to Ananias, 'Satan has given you a cold heart'. This is a lie told to the Holy Spirit, you did not give us all of the money. It was you and Sapphira who sold the property. It was your decision. It was your money to donate. How could you do this? You lied to God. Ananias collapsed, dead, on the floor. The people aware of it were frightened. Ananias was buried. Then that same day his wife appears. She was unaware of what happened'. Peter asked her, Was this the full amount for the property? 'Yes' was her answer. How could the two of you deny that which is the Lord's. The men who buried your husband will carry you out. "I do not understand,' said Sapphira. Then she died. She was buried beside her husband. A fear went throughout the church'.*"

"We should all be grateful this does not happen today as there would be no one in the real estate business. '*A fear went throughout the church'*, is the way the bishops, archbishops, and cardinals, want it to be. Keep 'em scared, keep 'em loyal, and keep 'em tithing. Christianity is not a revealed-religion of any god, it is a 'revealed-religion' that claims that if one does not believe as the church dictates; well, you know the supposed result. Now, let's finish with a little potpourri."

"Upon the birth of Jesus, an angel supposedly appears to shepherds described as 'lowly' in the Catholic scriptures. The angel told them about the birth of Christ. Why is being a shepherd lowly?"

"Scholars rearranged the birth of Jesus to be 6 BC; thus, adjusting the calendar, so that Herod's orders for a census would seem correct. Herod died in 4 BC. So, Jesus was born before Anno Domini. How can that be?"

"The 'wise men' were royal astrologers."

"Jesus describes the self-righteous showmen as hypocrites of false piety. They were first century televangelists. Sorry."

"I know you intend no insult," said Grace. "Please, continue."

"Easter is not mentioned in The New Testament. Easter is but a springtime festival of pagan fertility rites, and Easter is the fertility goddess."

"Paul's letter to the Romans gave the Calvinists the doctrine of predestination and Augustine the notion of original sin."

"Paul did not allow women to speak in church."

"Moses and Elijah supposedly appeared to Jesus about his impending death."

"So, then, who is the God of The New Testament, a Roman Catholic or a Protestant, or both? The New Testament is not as wrath-filled as The Tanach you may say. Ah, but I have not gotten to the last book of The New Testament. We will check out the wrath in the book entitled 'Revelation'. I feel it deserves a night or two of our discussion."

"That's it?" asked Grace.

"For tonight. Tomorrow night we will start on Revelation. After all, it has taken us three nights to get through The New Testament. It may well take us a couple of nights for Revelation. In a hurry? Gone somewhere?" laughed Zeus.

"I do have a lot of things to look-up. Okay, I'll be waiting for you. Good night" said Grace.

"Good night," said Zeus.

CHAPTER ELEVEN

GRACE'S REVELATION

"Grace, would you like to share," asked Ginny.

"I wasn't going to, but I think I will," began Grace, "since we have been on the topic of religion for the past weeks. I seemed to have brought that on. Except for group this morning, I have spent the day studying The Book of Revelation. Actually, last night I was going over it in my head. In seminary, we studied it, but I never 'really' studied it, if you catch my drift. It is amazing how little fault I found with the Bible ... the Protestant Old and New Testaments that is. We even studied The Book of Mormon, not to mention Hindu and Buddhist writings. Actually, we just brushed over them. We also studied the Catholic Bible with the Apocrypha inserted, unlike the Protestant scriptures."

"Just consider John of Patmos, John the third person writer of the 4th Gospel, John the writer of the epistles, and later calling himself 'Saint John', he supposedly wrote The Book of Revelation. Before he was called to heaven, John was supposedly banished to Patmos by order of the Roman Emperor Domitian who ruled around 81 to 96 AD. It was written that Domitian ruled 64 years after Jesus ascended, but this would make the post-ascension time period, with adjustments to the calendar, around 87 to 105 AD. However, within The Book of Revelation is a cryptic reference to Nero who reigned around 54 to 68 AD. Also, you will find that there is a reference in Revelation of that book being written in the 4th century AD."

"At the beginning of Revelation, John, whichever one he is, meets Jesus right off the bat. What I am going to talk about is what John encountered after being swift into heaven by an angel."

"In Revelation 1:12-16 you will find John writing in the first person, '*And I turned towards the voice. There I saw seven golden candlesticks. In the middle of this array I saw the son of man, wearing a golden girdle over a long robe. His hair was likened unto snow. His eyes were fire and his feet were molten brass. His voice was the flow of cascading water. In his right hand I saw seven stars. A two-edged sword protruded from his mouth. A bright light shined around him giving him power'*."

"In Revelation 1:20 John wrote, '*and the seven candlesticks represent the seven churches'*. Supposedly, Jesus gave John directions to write the seven churches words from the epistles of Paul."

"In Revelation 2:1 Jesus says, '*Unto the angel of the church of Ephesus write'* and from 2:4 Jesus says, '*I am somewhat against you, for you have left your charity which first above all'*."

"Jesus said as it is written in Revelation 2:8, '*And to the angel of Smyrna write'*, from 2:10, '*The devil will put some of you in prison to be tried. In there you will have ten days of tribulation. If you are faithful in your dying you will be given heaven'*."

"In Revelation 2:12 Jesus says, *'And to the angel of the church of Pergamus write'*. And from 2:14 Jesus continues, *'I have against your church things that are wroth as you have beheld the doctrine of Balaam and it was Balac that cast a wall separating the children of Israel who your church directed to commit fornication'*."

"In 2:18 John writes of Jesus saying, *'And to the angel of the church of Thyatira write, 'But a have things against you, because of Jezebel, as she thinks she is a prophetess, she teaches and subdues my people, to worship idols with sacrifices, and they fornicate. She was to confess her sins. If I cast her into your bed there will be a great tribulation, except if you confess. And I will bring death to her children and all the churches will know this'*. That can be found in 2:20-23."

"In 3:1,3 John writes that Jesus said, *'To the angel of the church of Sardis write … I know what you do. While you think you are alive, you are dead. I will be as a thief, and you will not know when I will come'*."

"From 3:7,9 Jesus says, *'To the angel of the church of Philadelphia write … my father has the key of David and what my father opens will not be shut and what my father shuts will not be opened. It is I who will bring the synagogue of the Devil'*."

"And to the 7th and last church John writes of Jesus saying in 3:14-18. *'And to the church of Laodicea write … I am aware of your work and you are of the middle faith and because you are only warm in your belief I will spit you out. You say you are rich and in need of nothing, but you are miserable, poor, naked, and without sight as you do not see what is before you. Buy me gold and then you will be made rich. And, you will cover your nakedness with fine clothes. And put salve in your eyes to see'*."

"Excuse me," said Ginny. "I hate to interrupt, but how can you know all of this. How could you have memorized all of it … all the verses."

"It was given to me last night and I remember all the words. I remember all the words given me in the night," replied Grace.

"How are you given this in the night?" asked Ginny.

"If I told you that, you would lock me up here forever," laughed Grace.

"Okay, I won't ask you. Please, continue," said Ginny.

"First charity, tithe first, then tribulation for ten days, death; Balaam, fornication; Jezebel, fornication; they are dead, Jesus comes as a thief; warm in faith, buy Jesus gold. The wrath has begun with Jesus and a double-edged sword coming out of his mouth."

"Let's proceed to the seven seals. Keep in mind the creatures and monsters as I talk about them."

"Revelation 5:1, 'In the right hand of Jesus was a book containing the seven seals'. And onto 5:5-6. 'An elder said to them here is the lion of Judah and of David, and the seven seals will be freed. And in the midst of the throne were 'four creatures' and a 'dead lamb with seven horns and seven eyes', as these are the 'seven spirits of God'. And, in 5:11, 'Many angels sang and I heard them and the 'living creatures' and the elders in numbers of thousands'."

"Okay, there are a lot of sevens. You will understand this as we move along. Seven is a number used coincidental with the 'seven spirits of God'. John just wrote of the seven spirits of God, but never went on the explain them."

"I think I have talked enough. I've taken up thirty minutes already. Besides, that's all I heard last night. I am sure I am going to hear more tonight," said Grace.

"Doris, you haven't shared in a long time. Would you like to?" asked Ginny.

"This is scary. I mean, I am scared right now. I don't know what to do. I never read that stuff in the Bible. I mean, we have a Bible, my husband and I, but I'm ashamed to say, I have never picked it up. I don't think my husband has either. It's just in the house. I think we got it because it is good to have a Bible in the house. Anyway, that is all I have to say," said Doris.

"Becca, how about you?" asked Ginny.

"Okay," began Becca. "Yesterday, Doctor Phelps diagnosed me with schizophrenia. You think that Revelation stuff scares you. I've come to realize that I am going to have voices in my head for the remainder of my life. I am terrified. Doctor Phelps said my meds should kick in in two weeks. Great, I have to be in here two more weeks and if the meds aren't working … well … I have to be here longer. I feel like this place is going to be my permanent address."

"Frankly, I don't care about the seven seals or whatever. I guess we get the four horses next. Let's see, there is the pink horse, the yellow horse, the baby-blue horse, and I guess the fuchsia horse. It's all a bunch of stuff, just stuff, to scare people. Schizophrenia is scary. I'll deal with that scare for a while."

"Okay gang, time is up. I'll be waiting to see you tomorrow morning. Nine on the dot," said Ginny. "Can you stay a minute, Grace?"

"Sure," said Grace. "Do you want to go to your office?"

"No, we'll wait a minute when everyone has left, and we can talk here," replied Ginny. "All right, all gone."

"You are going to ask about the voice in my head, aren't you?" asked Grace.

"Yes, let me in a little and tell me about it," said Ginny.

"I will tell you just a little," said Grace.

<<<>>>

"Hi Grace. Laid it all out there this morning ... did you not?"

"Well, hello. And, yes, I did. Wanted to hit them with Revelation. As you probably know the most read book of the Bible is Genesis ... people quit reading after that. And, of course you know the highest selling book in the United States is the Bible. Do you know the second highest selling book in the United States?" asked Grace.

"Atlas Shrugged ... Ayn Rand. It is the second highest selling book and is read by more folks than the Bible. Of course, you knew that," said Zeus.

"Yes, I did. I was just seeing if you had a handle on it," said Grace.

"Grace, I have a handle on everything," replied Zeus.

"I guess I knew that," said Grace.

"Okay, get ready for some more Revelation," said Zeus. "Let's go to Zechariah before we get into the sevens of this and that."

"Zechariah is the next to the last book of The Christian Old Testament. I don't remember a thing about Zechariah," said Grace.

"I imagine you don't. So, I will catch you up on ol' Zech. Go to 6:1-7 after you wake up. Zechariah is writing, 'Now I lifted up my eyes again and looked, and behold, four chariots were coming toward me out of the valley. And the mountains above the valley were bronze. Red horses pulled the first chariot, and with the second chariot were black horses in the reins, and white horses with the third chariot, and the fourth chariot, dappled horses. And I asked the angel who was speaking to me, Why these chariots? And, the angel said to me, 'These are four spirits come from heaven. They stood before the Lord. The black horses are going North and the white horses will follow them. The dappled horses will go to the South, all to survey the Earth'," said Zeus.

"What about the red horses? Where did they go?" asked Grace.

"Beats me. It doesn't say. So, let's go on to The Book of Revelation, 6:1-8. John wrote. 'The Lamb opened the seven seals and one of the four creatures thundered, 'Look'. I did see and I saw a white horse. The Lamb was riding the horse and carrying a bow and wearing a crown that He may conquer. On the white horse was the Lamb, the Christ going out to fulfill the Gospels and conquer the Earth. The other horses are the judgement and punishment that will befall the enemies of the Christ. War is the red horse, starvation is the black horse, and of the pale horse it is pestilence, plagues, and death to the rider. And that was the opening of the first seal. I went and I saw

114

that another horse went out. And the horse's rider will take all peace from the Earth and man will kill man. And that was the opening of the second seal. And, when the third seal was opened I saw a black horse, and scales were in the hands of the rider. Then a voice rang out that two pounds of wheat for a penny, and three times that of barley for but a penny, and we were not to destroy any wine or oil. And, I saw a pale horse with the opening of the fourth seal. Hell followed him and he was called death. The rider had power over the Earth and was to sow famine, and use the beasts to kill'," said Zeus.

"Whew. That settles the equine problem. It appears to be copied form Zechariah," said Grace.

"It is. 'The Lamb or Jesus opened the first seal and then rode away with a bow in his hand and a crown on his head. So, it begs the question as to who opened the other seals? Killing, pestilence, famine, and death is the beginning," said Zeus. "When the 5th seal is opened there is found under the alter those that were killed for the word of God. And, in Revelations 6:10 it is written, *'They screamed and asked the Lord how long will this go on oh Lord? Do you not protect those who are holy and steadfast? They asked out of love for the Lord and held nothing against their enemies'.*"

"Now, we are reading about revenge and not taking it out of love for God. But, only the Lord can send someone to avenge the believers. Now, before we get to the 6th and 7th seal, the seven trumpets and the seven vials, we are going to list the ten plagues on Egypt that God made them suffer before the Pharaoh would let Moses' people go."

"The ten plagues ... from Exodus?" asked Grace.

"Exactly," replied Zeus "Follow along. Exodus 7:14-24, water into blood."

"Exodus 7:14 to 8:15; frogs."

"Exodus 8:16-19; lice."

"Exodus 8:20-32; wild animals."

"Exodus 9:1-7; diseased livestock."

"Exodus 9:8-12; boils."

"Exodus 9:13-35; thunderstorms of hail."

"Exodus 10:1-20; locusts."

"Exodus 10:21-29; darkening for three days."

"Exodus 11:1-2,36; death of the first born."

"The reason I am listing these, is you will find the plagues in the seven seals, the seven trumpets, and in the seven vials. Of course, along with the four horsemen taken from Zechariah."

"Okay, to Revelation 6:12 '*And I saw, as the 6th seal was opened there was a great quaking of the Earth. And, the moon became blood red*'."

"And, onto Revelation 6:17, '*Their wrath has come. Who will live?*"

"All right, the 6th seal is opened and '*their wrath has come*' is referring to the horsemen, one of which is Jesus. Before we get to the 7th seal, remember this. There is, of course, 12 tribes of Israel. Out of those tribes, Jesus selects 12,000 from each having then 144,000; all men. This 144,000 were to be saved from the wrath of God. All of those chosen have marks placed on their heads."

"So, let's go to Revelation 7:3-4, *'We will seal those of the tribes with a mark on their foreheads. Until then do not show your power over the wooded land, the waters, and the Earth. I know of what they say, those 144,000, for they are the sons of Israel.'*"

"Sons of Israel … all men," said Grace.

"Correct. And the *'we'* at the beginning of the verse is not explained. It could be John and God, John and Jesus, or Jesus and his father. Plus, anyone of the 12 tribes not chosen are killed. Leaving only men to survive. Ol' John was not thinking ahead when he wrote this," said Zeus."

"Let's go to Revelation 8:1-2, *'And when he opened the 7th seal all was quiet for half an hour. I saw angels standing with God, and they each had in their right hand a trumpet'*," said Zeus.

"Whew. This is like learning this stuff all over again," said Grace.

"In your fundamentalist seminary you were taught it the way 'they' wanted you to preach it. You were even taught that the creation story was science," said Zeus.

"I know that. I was always a bit skeptical of that. Eve from the rib and all," said Grace.

"We will touch on that tomorrow night. So, for now, good night Grace."

"Good night, Zeus."

CHAPTER TWELVE

TRUMPETS AND VIALS

"Where are you?"

"Right here. I had something to do first," said Zeus.

"How could you possibly have something … oh … never mind," said Grace.

"Aren't we testy tonight," laughed Zeus.

"I'm sort of mad at myself," said Grace.

"Por que?" asked Zeus.

"Why? I'll tell you why. I have read the whole Bible and realize now that I have only studied the 'good stuff'." That's why," replied Grace.

"What I am giving you is the proof as to why you have doubted after all these years. Yes, you did only look at the 'good stuff', but when you came to realize that just the good stuff was not enough, you turned your back on it all. But, you still have a little spark, a tiny ember of belief. Don't you?" asked Zeus.

"A tiny ember is a good way to describe it. I just can't extinguish it," said Grace.

"When we finish our search for the truth, you will be able to extinguish your ember of doubt," said Zeus.

"More Revelation? I guess we are about finished?" said Grace.

"Not even close," replied Zeus.

"It's Revelation, the last book of the Bible," said Grace.

"We are going to go much further than that. Remember, you just told me of all that you studied in divinity school. The 'other' religions you studied. Well we have them to cover," said Zeus.

"Like I need Hinduism or Buddhism to study?" said Grace.

"Oh, but you do, or you will never be free of that last tiny ember," said Zeus.

"Okay. I trust you and I can't say I trust that last tiny ember," said Grace.

"Enough of this. Let's get on to the seven trumpets," said Zeus.

"I am ready," replied Grace.

"Revelation 8:1-2," began Zeus. *'And the first angel blew the trumpet and cast to the earth was bloody fire and hail. A third of the Earth was burnt to ruin. And a third of the trees were on fire, and all the green grasses of the Earth were burnt'."*

"Revelation 9:8-9. *'And the second angel blew the trumpet and a huge mountain full of fire was cast into the waters. A third of the waters was full of blood. And a third of all creatures in the water were killed by it. And, a third of the ships on the waters were burnt up'."*

"Revelation 8:10-11. *'The third angel blew the trumpet and a star fell from heaven and it burned like a torch. The star fell on a third of the rivers and*

119

upon the fountains of the rivers. The name of the star was Wormwood. A third of the waters was to be called Wormwood. And, many were bitter and drowned'."

"Revelation 8:12. *'And the fourth angel blew the trumpet and a third of the sun was burnt out, as was a third of the moon, and as well a third of the stars. It was that a third of them were darkened. The sun, the moon, and the stars did not shine for a third part of the day and a third part of the night'."*

"Revelation 9:1-3. *'And the fifth angel blew his trumpet and I saw a star fall and it became a key to the bottomless pit. And by that key the angel was given the power to open hell. When he opened the pit a pall of smoke rose to the sky. The sun and the air were darkened. And locusts sprang from the pit. Power was given to the locusts as power had been given to the scorpions. The locusts flew out of the pit as devils for the Antichrist. They appeared as large locusts, some as big as monsters, but they were assuredly locusts. And the locusts came to torment those not of the 144,000'."*

"The 144,000 were saved. So far, with the seals and the trumpets, two thirds of all humankind have been killed. But get this. In Revelation 9:4 John wrote *'And it was commanded of the 144,000 that no pain should come to all of the grasses of the Earth."* But, in Revelation 8:7 all the green grasses were burnt up. How can all the grass be in pain if it was all gone?" asked Zeus.

"I wondered about those verses that contradict one another," said Grace.

"Oh, we will cover all of that in due time," said Zeus. "Now, more about the locusts. Remember the locusts from the list we went over. Also, the earthquakes and the sun, the moon, and the stars being darkened. Right out of Exodus."

"Revelation 9:7-11. *'The locusts were as horses going to war. The horses had crowns on their heads. It was a golden crown and they looked like men. They had lions' teeth and hair as a woman would have. They wore iron breastplates and they flew. The horses' wings made the noise of war. The locusts had stingers like scorpions. For half a year the locusts were to cause pain to the subjects of the angel of the bottomless pit'.*"

<<<>>>

"You hear voices?" asked Doris.

"Not exactly ... not voices. I do hear one voice," replied Grace.

"What is Doctor Phelps going to do?" asked Doris.

"Not load me up on meds ... I hope," replied Grace.

"I think Doctor Phelps and Thelma are going to tell me I am a schizophrenic. And then, as you say, they are going to load me up on meds. They told me I would be leaving soon, but now this. I have no idea how long I will be here," said Doris.

"Do you hear voices?" asked Grace.

"I think so. I only hear them when I am sleeping, but I told Thelma I don't hear any voices. Do you think I should come clean with her?" asked Doris.

"That's when I hear my voice, too. And yes, you should 'come clean', as you say," replied Grace. "I thought the voices were dreams at first ... but ... the same voice keeps coming back ... night after night."

"Okay, I'm going to go to Thelma's office right now. If she has a patient with her, I'll wait 'til she is done with the session. I feel better already. Thanks, Grace," said Doris.

"Good for you. Atta girl," said Grace.

"Oh, one more question," said Doris. "Have you told Thelma about your voice?"

"Didn't need to. I shared it in group and Ginny told Thelma," said Grace.

"Oh, my. Ginny ratted you out," said Doris.

"I guess you could look at it that way," said Grace. "Good luck with Thelma."

"See you later," said Doris.

<<<>>>

"Grace. Grace."

"Zeus. Zeus."

"We are going to have a short night tonight," said Zeus

"Why?" asked Grace.

"Well, I don't want to get into the first creation story, the Antichrist and the seven vials. We can go over that tomorrow night," replied Zeus.

"Sounds good to me. I am all ears," said Grace. "The first creation story? It seems I don't know jack about this Bible from which I was preaching."

"Perhaps not. Okay on to Revelation 9:13-19, *'And the sixth angel blew his horn. Then the four golden horns of the alter spoke with God present, saying the sixth angel with the trumpet was to set loose the four angels who were held in the Euphrates river. The four angels were set free and they were prepared to kill one third of all mankind. And the number of an army 2,000,000. And I saw the angel on a horse wearing a breastplate of fire and brimstone. The heads of the horses were the heads of lions. And the lions spit out fire and brimstone. And a third part of humankind was destroyed and none lived. And the angels rode away on their horses. And their horses had tails of a serpent,*" said Zeus.

"Thus, the only ones left on the planet were the ones with the mark ... the 144,000. These verses beg the question, why have an army of millions if the four angels on horses with lion's heads killed them all by killing the last third of all humankind?" said Zeus.

"Those verses are very confusing," said Grace.

"Oh, 'you ain't heard nothin' yet,' as Al Jolson once said. Let's continue with the sixth angel with Revelation 11:3-8, *'Here are two who are witnesses and prophets, and who for three and a half years wore sackcloth. They stand before the God of the Earth. If anyone conspires to harm them they will spit out fire and devour them those that conspire must be killed. They can close heaven so that it will not rain while they prophesize. They will turn water into blood and will bring about plagues as they will. When they complete their prophesizing, they shall be killed by a beast from the*

123

Earth. And their bodies will lay in rest in a grand city which is the spirit of Sodom and Egypt where Jesus was crucified'," said Zeus.

"Why all the killing if all are dead, save those with the mark, the 12,000 from each of the 12 tribes? Sodom is not a grand city and Egypt is a country. According to the myth, Jesus was crucified, died, buried, and was resurrected in Sodom or Egypt, none of which is in the books before Revelation. Okay we will still have a bit of the sixth trumpet to go."

"Revelation 11:13. *'... there was an earthquake and a small part of the city was destroyed. And there, slain in the earthquake some 7,000 and the rest became afraid and prayed to God'*," said Zeus.

"Everyone has been killed, or were the 7,000 a part of those with the mark? The writer of this book seems to have a problem with continuity. In Revelation 11:15 it reads, *'And the seventh angel blew the trumpet. And there were voices speaking to the people from heaven saying the Lord and the Christ will reign forever. Amen'*. And in 11:19 it goes, *'And in heaven was the temple and it was opened by God, and in the temple was an ark and in the ark was God's testament. And there was an earthquake with lightening and hail, and there were voices crying out'*," said Zeus.

"Enough with the earthquakes, already!" said Grace.

"I agree," said Zeus. "There is no originality in Revelation. The horsemen, the plagues, and the constant killing are all reminiscent of The Tanach and are no doubt derived from stories passed down through the centuries, not written, but by word of mouth."

"That's it, goodnight," said Zeus.

"But wait ... darn," replied Grace.

<<<>>>

"**In Revelation ...**"

"Whoa, just a minute. Let me focus a little bit before you start," said Grace.

"**Okay. Take your time,**" replied Zeus.

"Alright, proceed ... in Revelation ..." said Grace.

"**In Revelation 12:3-6 it reads, '*There was another sign in heaven. A great red dragon with seven heads appeared, it had ten horns and on its heads there were seven jeweled crowns. His tail threw a third of the stars in the heavens onto the Earth. And the dragon came to the woman who was about to deliver a child; a son that she might devour. And born to her was a man child who will take an iron rod and rule the nations. God took up the Son to his thrown. The woman ran away out into the wilderness, were God had a place for her, and that she would be fed for three and a half years'.*"**

"**The woman fleeing into the wilderness is reminiscent of the first wife of Adam. There are two stories of God creating man and woman,**" said Zeus.

"Yes, I am aware of that," said Grace.

"**I have saved that from the Tanach,**" said Zeus.

"Genesis 1:27," said Grace.

"**Spot on,**" said Zeus. **And it reads, '*And God created Man in his likeness, He created them male and female'.*"**

"Now to Genesis 2:21-22," said Grace.

"Again, correct," said Zeus. And it reads, '*God cast the man into a deep sleep, while sleeping, from the man's side did He take a rib. From the rib God created a woman, then He wakened the man so he could see the woman standing next to him'.*"

"Now we will delve into the first creation story. The story of the woman Lilith, or Lili in Hebrew. Lilith is a figure in Jewish mythology, developed earliest in the Babylonian Talmud, around the 3rd to 5th century. Lilith is a dangerous demon of the night. She is sexually wanton. And, she steals babies in the darkness. In Hebrew language texts Lilith translates to night creature, or night monster, or night hag, or screech owl."

"Isaiah 34:14 reads, '*The desert creatures will meet the wolves. A hairy goat will cry out. There will be the night monster who has found a place to rest'.*"

"Lilith left Adam as she refused to be subservient to him. The Lilith legend continues to serve as source material in Western culture, literature, occultism, fantasy, and horror. You will see in the next verses how the legend of Lilith from Genesis could have continued to The Book of Revelation. Later in our review there will be some indication that Revelation could have been written in the 4th century of the common era."

"Let's go to Revelation 12:12-14, '*A warning a devil will come down upon the Earth with wrath. The devil knows his time is short. And the devil prosecuted the woman who bore the man child. The woman was given wings of an eagle to fly into the desert and there shall she live'.* The devil that comes down is the Antichrist. First God took the man child up to his throne and there created the Antichrist who would rule for three and a half years. Instead of a screech owl, our lady of the desert is given the wings of an eagle. Now, back to the seven-headed beast."

"Revelation 13:1 finds John writing in the third person, '*And a beast rose from the sea. It had seven heads and ten horns and on the horns were crown jewels, and on his heads were the names of blasphemy*'."

"This monster is a bit different as it has '*the names of blasphemy*' on the heads. The seven heads of the monster could represent the seven kingdoms of Egypt, Assyria, Chaldea, Persia, Greece, the city of Rome, and the empire of the Antichrist. The Antichrist is not worldwide but is probably limited to Israel, which is not mentioned as one of the seven kingdoms. We will discover as we go along that the seven heads could represent something else. Now, onto another monster."

"Revelation 13:2-3, '*The beast I saw was a leopard with the feet of a bear and the mouth of a lion. He was given great power by the dragon. His head wound had caused his death but then it was healed. And all the Earth admired the beast*'."

"The mortal wound was because of the idolatry of the Roman Empire and the wound was given the monster by the Roman Catholic Emperor Constantine. If that is so, then The Book of Revelation could not have been written until the 4th century AD. Constantine ruled from 306 until 337 AD."

"Revelation 13:11, '*I witnessed a monster coming up from the Earth, with two horns like a lamb and when he spoke it was with the dragon's voice*'."

"Wait. Lambs don't have horns. One must ask the question, Why so many monsters?" asked Grace.

"Revelation 13:13-18, *'The Antichrist will make a mark on those great and small, wealthy or poor, those free and enslaved, to show on their right hand or forehead. No man can sell a slave and as with all the slaves will have the name and number of the beast. For he who has wisdom let the number of the beast be counted. It will be the number of man and the number will be 666'.*"

"Letters are used in Hebrew to represent numbers as with aleph is one, bet is two and so on. If you transpose the letters in Hebrew to the name of Emperor Nero, you will come up with 666. Nero ruled from 54 until 68 AD."

"The marks on the right hand and the forehead are known as the mark of the beast. Follow along in Revelation 14:9-11, *'And the third angel spoke in a loud voice as he followed them telling them that anyone who follows the beast will have the wrath of God and he will be tormented with fire in the sight of the Lamb. And the smoke of their torment will rise ever higher and higher, and those who adore the beast will have no rest'.*"

"Who are these people that are put upon by God? The only people walking the Earth are the 144,000; all men. Okay, let's move onto the Vials."

"More wrath," said Grace.

"Indeed, now let's go to Revelation 15:1,7, *'And there was a wonderful sign in heaven. Seven angels descended carrying the last of the seven plagues filled with the wrath of God. And a living creature gave a vial, each to the seven angels. The vials were filled with the wrath of God'."*

"Let's continue with the seven vials and see how much they match the ten plagues upon Egypt. Revelation 16:2-4, *'The first angel poured his vial upon the Earth. And boils were upon those with the mark of the beast. And the second poured his vial into the oceans and there was blood and all in the oceans died. And the third angel poured out his vial into the streams and rivers and turned them to blood'."*

"Revelation 16:8, *'And the fourth angel poured his vial on the sun and burned those with the mark with fire'."*

"Revelation 16:10, *'The fifth angel poured his vial upon the beast and the beast's kingdom darkened'."*

"Revelation 16:12-13, *'The sixth angle poured out his vial into the Euphrates that the sun might reign and I saw from the mouth of the prophet three unclean frogs'."*

"Revelation 16:17, *'The seventh angel strew his vial into the air and from the throne of God there came a voice saying; all is done'."*

"That is the end of the plagues. Later on, in the 17th chapter, the 7 heads of the beast measure up to the 7 hills of Rome. No emperor is written down to give us a time line. And in chapter 20, God sends the Antichrist, described as the devil into a pit for a thousand years. Thus, one must assume the devil will be let loose after the thousand years. So, God the holy spirit, and Jesus will reign over the Earth for a thousand years. Why only a thousand years? Ah, but the wrath continues."

"Revelation 21:8, *'The whoremongers, the unbelievers, the liars, and the murderers will be cast into the fire, for a second death'.*"

"Revelation 22:5, *'And there will be no light as the Lord will enlighten them to reign forever'.*"

"And now we come to the end with this last wrath filled verse, Revelation 22:18, *'I warn everyone not to change a word of this book for surely God will rain down plagues upon them that do so'.*"

"Whew, rough book, said Grace.

"Let's wrap it up and then I'll let you go," said Zeus.

"So, we are coming to the end of The New Testament?" asked Grace.

"Yes," said Zeus. "In the last verse I quoted, John or whomever wrote the book, is telling the reader that if anyone changes even a word of Revelation, God will rain down plagues upon them such as those of the seven seals, the seven trumpets, and the seven vials. Oy, what chutzpah. So, now God administers copyrights."

"Whoever wrote this book was mean, cruel, a hater of women as he considered them all to be whores or evil, as with the mother of the Antichrist. The writer was filled with wrath, much as were the writers of The Tanach. Thus, the writers of The Books of The New Testament are not only fundamentalists of their revealed-religion, they substantiate that the God they depict is their God alone and they know best for those that read the threats. The threats of hell and mankind being wiped out in the last days are threats to keep the flock in line."

"Let's do a little potpourri," said Zeus.

"Good, I like potpourri," replied Grace.

"Daniel had a dream of four beasts, a winged lion, a bear, a four-headed winged leopard, and a ten-horned beast. Seems the writer of Revelation took a bit from The Tanach."

"The Messiah is described in The Book of Daniel as having white hair and a fiery appearance. Again, from The Tanach to Revelation."

During the Reformation Protestants believed the Pope was the Antichrist."

"The 6th letter in Hebrew is 'w', making 'www', 666."

"The Tanach and The New Testament are not the works of the people who were supposed to have written them as some of those books would not have been written in the third person. The Books were approved by Roman Catholic clergy when they decided what to place in the Bible in 367 AD. Thus, we end The New Testament. Take tomorrow night off. I will be here the next day. Bye," said Zeus.

"Bye," replied Grace.

CHAPTER THIRTEEN

ONLY THE DELIGHTSOME MAY APPLY

"Thelma wants to see you," said Lorna.

"But it's almost time for group," said Grace.

"She said you can miss group. You can go to the four o'clock group," said Lorna.

"Okay, I'll get on the way," said Grace.

"Have a good session," replied Lorna.

<<<>>>

"Hi Grace. Come right in. I know I am taking you away from group. Tell me. If you were in group what would you share today, if I may ask?" said Thelma.

"I was going to share a bit about what I am learning. I was going to talk about Zeus. He gave me permission to do that," said Grace.

"Zeus. The voice in your head?" asked Thelma.

"Yes. And the funny thing is … well … I remember every word he said. I even remember our little conversations that have nothing to do with scripture," said Grace.

"Word for word?" asked Thelma.

"Word for word," replied Grace.

"It's been two weeks since we put you on lamotrigine," said Thelma.

"The mood stabilizer?" asked Grace.

"It will soon be kicking in," replied Thelma.

"I hope it does not erase the voice. I need Zeus. I would say I need Zeus for another month," said Grace.

"Why?" asked Thelma.

"We are essentially talking about the things I separated from," said Grace.

"The church? Your religion?" asked Thelma.

"Yes. And the more we talk the more I am convinced I made the right decision," said Grace.

"So, you are starting to lose that little bit of faith you have?" asked Thelma.

"I am. That is why I don't want Zeus to go away," said Grace. "I believe he is the key to my recovery."

"Recovery. To return to your faith? I don't understand," said Thelma.

"No, no, no ... not to return, but to finally lose that little flicker of faith I have," said Grace.

"What are you going to do when you lose all of your faith ... lose that little flicker?" asked Thelma.

"I am going to turn my back on the whole thing. The university. The television. The president's council. All of it," said Grace.

"What will you do? How will you make a living?" asked Thelma.

"I have plenty socked away. Televangelism is very lucrative. Plus, the schools board told me if need be they will buy out my contract ... I have three years to go and they are going to pay me for that. Essentially, they told me in not so many words that they really don't want a nut case back on the campus," said Grace.

"If televangelism was so lucrative how come you don't have a few mansions, a ski lodge in Vail, a private jet, and a humongous boat a hundred-feet long?" laughed Thelma.

"I found that to be disgusting. I didn't even want to be associated with them," said Grace. "I preached the gospel. I tried to give my flock hope in their lives. Oh, I collected money, but I never did the 'plant the seed' bit. I never told my worshipers to write a check for a thousand dollars. And, if they do they will get more money back in return. Ludicrous, and shameful ... and crooked. Someone on social security is to write a check for a grand in hopes of getting more in return. And, all because some rip-off artist posing as a minister tells them it is so. They have no shame and they certainly are not clergy. None of them."

Whew, let it all out," said Thelma.

"I have to when it comes to that. I may hear a voice in my head but I never 'spoke in tongues' either. That is ... well ... silly ... no ... ridiculous. Grown men and women jabbering as if they are channeling a spirit. Stupid," said Grace.

"So, back to Zeus. "You want to keep his voice going?" asked Thelma.

"Really, I do. I am learning so much. Zeus is good for me. I fear that someday he will be gone. I will be broken hearted," said Grace.

"Are you anxious about that? I can have Doctor Phelps write a script for anxiety," said Thelma.

"I don't think I need that," replied Grace.

"Okay. You'll let me know if you feel you need it," said Thelma.

"I will. I promise," replied Grace.

"I wanted to see how you are doing. This may sound like a funny question. Will you let me know when the flicker of faith is extinguished?" asked Thelma.

"I will. As soon as I know, you will know. Again, I promise," replied Grace.

"Alright, that will do it for today," said Thelma.

"Thanks. I really enjoy talking to you. I feel comfortable around you … it's a certain warmth," said Grace.

"Thank-you, that was very kind. You are coming along very well. Things are looking up," said Thelma.

"May I give you a hug?" asked Grace.

"I'd love a hug," replied Thelma.

<<<>>>

"S'up, Happening'?" asked Zeus.

"Que paso, que cosa fi," replied Grace.

"Que cosa fi?" asked Zeus.

"Italian for what's happening," laughed Grace.

"Oh, now you are tri-lingual," said Zeus.

"Bitte, bitte," replied Grace.

"Okay, we have Europe covered," said Zeus.

"So, what is for tonight?" asked Grace.

"Joseph Smith and his books, starting with The Book of Mormon," replied Zeus.

"As William wrote, 'lead on McDuff," said Grace.

"The Book of Mormon, with the sub-title of, Another Testament of Jesus Christ, is one of the four books that define the Mormon revealed-religion. Mormons prefer to be referred to as being a member of The Church of Jesus Christ of Latter-day Saints, LDS. They refer to themselves as Latter Day Saints as each member of the LDS Church is recognized as a saint," said Zeus.

"One of the other books that serves as a companion to The Book of Mormon is an early book of Joseph Smith's prophesies called The Book of Commandments. Very few of the original volumes that he supposedly wrote survived, as rioters destroyed the presses of the publisher in 1833.

Only about 30 of the original copies survive today. A third book, Doctrines and Covenants, was published in 1835 and through the years has been edited by both the LDS Church officials and the Fundamentalist LDS Church or FLDS Church hierarchy. Pearl of Great Price was a work of Joseph Smith's published around 1842."

"One very noteworthy piece of information to know about the Mormon's founder is that it was doubtful if he could not read or write. So much of what I am going to tell you is beyond belief."

"In his History of the Church, Joseph Smith had it transcribed for himself the following, 'I have more to boast about than any other man had. I am the only man that has ever been able to keep a whole church together since the days of Adam. A large majority of the whole have stood by me. Neither Paul, John, Peter, nor Jesus ever did it. I boast that no man ever did such a work as I. The followers of Jesus ran away from him; but the Latter-day Saints never ran away from me, yet'."

"Humble, he was not. Let's look into the life of this ego run wild, Joseph Smith," continued Zeus.

"On December 23, 1805, Joseph Smith Junior was born in Sharon, Vermont."

"In 1816 Joseph's family moved to Manchester, New York, near Palmyra."

"And, in 1820 at the very young age of 15 Smith claims a vision in which he was visited by two personages, God and Jesus in physical bodies. Smith had someone else write for him, 'So, in accordance with this, my determination to ask God, I retired to the woods to make an attempt.

When the light rested upon me, I saw two personages, whose brightness and glory defy all description, standing above me in the air. One of them spake unto me, calling me by name and said pointing to the other ... 'This is my beloved son. Hear Him!',"

"How do we know he had all of this transcribed? I say transcribed as there is no proof that Joseph Smith was literate. Smith had transcribed, 'My object in going to inquire of the Lord was to know which of all the sects was right, that I might know which to join. I asked the personages who stood above me in the light, which of all the sects was right, for at this time it had never entered into my heart that all were wrong, and which I should join. I was answered that I must join none of them, for they were all wrong. The personage who addressed me said that all their creeds were an abomination in his sight; that those professors were all corrupt; that: as God said, 'They drew near to me with their lips, but their hearts are far from me, they teach for doctrines and commandments of men'. Here he denounces all other religions, supposedly when he was only 15 years old."

"In 1823, Smith said he had been visited by the angel Moroni. Moroni supposedly revealed to him the location of golden plates and other sacred items. Along with the golden plates was a breastplate with two seer stones known as Urim and Thummim. Urim and Thummim were just names made up by Smith. This is important to remember for later on. Smith was only 18 when he said he was visited by Moroni."

"In 1826, when Smith tried to sell the stones as buried treasure, he was brought trial on behalf of those that hired him. Smith was put on trial for using a seer stone of glass to defraud. The outcome of the trial is unknown."

"In 1827, a month after Smith married Emma Hale, they moved to Harmony, Pennsylvania. Penniless Smith had to borrow money from his neighbor, Martin Harris."

"In Smith's transcripts, in 1828, he explains that after four annual visitations to the sight of the golden plates, the breastplate, and the seer stones, the angel Moroni allowed Smith to possess the items. Supposedly, he just kept them without yet showing them to anyone."

"Martin Harris arrived at the Smith home to assist in transcribing the golden plates with writings on them. Smith dictated the golden plates by reading the seer stones in a hat from a language Smith identified as reformed Egyptian."

"Harris's wife was leery of the transcriptions. Smith allowed the transcriptions, thus far 116 pages, to be taken home by Harris for his wife to read. All 116 pages were either lost or destroyed. Smith had to have them transcribed all over again."

"Due to the loss of the 116 pages, the angel Maroni took away the plates and Smith's ability to have them transcribed. However, the plates were eventually returned and when Smith began the recitation to repeat the first 116 pages. They were nothing like the original transcription."

"In 1829, the transcriptions were completed."

"On two occasions, first three and then eight men were allowed to see the golden plates and each group attested to the witnessing of the plates in writing. With Smith, the witnesses to the golden plates numbered 12. Ah, 12, again."

"John the Baptist supposedly appeared to Smith, and a man named Oliver Cowdery, to take them into the fold of the Aaronic priesthood. A month later, Smith claimed to have been visited by the apostles Peter, James, and John upon which Smith entered the priesthood of Melchizedek."

"In 1830, The Book of Mormon, translated from the golden plates was published."

"The locals did not take to Mormonism very well and staged a number of plots which led to Smith being a disorderly person. The outcome of these events is unknown."

"Cowdery was sent out by Smith to find the New Jerusalem. Cowdery found it in Jackson County, Missouri."

"In 1831, Smith declared that Independence, Missouri was the center place of Zion."

"Even though the New Jerusalem was in Missouri, Smith was now living in Ohio."

"In 1833, mobs attacked the Mormons in their community of Zion, evicted them and destroyed their property. In the riot, one Mormon and two non-Mormons were killed."

"In 1835, a mob in Ohio attacked Smith, tarred and feathered him and left him for dead."

"Smith still resided in Kirkland, Ohio where a Mormon temple was built. Smith then organized five leadership groups including the Quorum of Apostles, there number being 12."

"Like the earthquakes, enough with the 12 already," laughed Grace.

"Indeed. In 1837, Smith and a Mormon named Rigdon entered into an enterprise of a stock company called Kirkland Safety Society. It failed the first month erasing the life savings of many investors. A warrant was issued for Smith charging him with fraud. Smith escaped to Missouri."

"In 1838, Smith moved his flock to the new Zion in Far West, Missouri. It was not long until an anti-Mormon group, who dubbed themselves the Danites, expelled the Mormons from Far West."

"Known as the battle of Crooked River, the battle took place as Governor Lilburn Boggs ordered the Mormons to be exterminated or driven from the state. Smith was captured, brought to trial, found guilty of treason, and was ordered to be hanged the next day. A general in the Missouri militia refused to carry out the order."

"The president of the Quorum of Apostles, Brigham Young, relocated 14,000 if his Mormon saints to Illinois and Iowa."

"In the meantime, Smith was still in custody for treason, but managed to escape from the Davis County jail with the help of his jailers."

"In 1839, Smith moved what was left of his Mormon saints to Commerce, Illinois. The town was renamed Nauvoo, which in Hebrew means, 'to be beautiful'."

"In 1840, Smith introduces baptism for the dead; thus, creating Mormon spirits out of non-Mormon dead."

"In 1841, Smith orders the restoration of the Aaronic and Melchizedek priesthoods."

"However, Smith did not have the first account of this vision quoted above until 1842. It was not until 1840 that Smith even started talking about his revelation. Smith, however, spoke of another account later on, that described only the Lord Jesus visiting him. A total contradiction to his 1842 revelation published in 1842. Around 1831 Smith had transcribed that he was visited by many angels, instead of God and Jesus that he originally told of. Smith, further stated, contradicting himself again, that he was visited by an angel in his bedroom."

"In 1843, Smith becomes a candidate for president of the United States."

"In 1844, Smith devises a first anointing with secret handshakes and codewords similar to Masonic rites. Smith's doctrine of many gods was published. Smith, along with his brother Hyrum, were arrested for treason and taken to the Carthage, Missouri jail. On 27 June, a mob formed to break into the jail, did so, and killed Smith and his brother."

"In 1847, to escape religious persecution, Brigham Young took his flock West to Utah, and they settled in Salt Lake City."

"Smith attracted thousands of devoted followers before his death in 1844 and millions in the century that followed. Among Mormons, he is regarded as a prophet on par with Moses and Elijah. In the 2015 compilation of the one hundred significant Americans of all time, the

Smithsonian magazine ranked Smith first in the category of religious figures. More nuanced interpretations range from viewing Smith as a prophet who had normal human weaknesses; a pious fraud who believed he was called by God to preach repentance and felt justified inventing visions in order to convert people; or a gifted mythmaker who was a product of his Yankee environment."

"Most anti-Mormon books face-off between The Book of Mormon, The Tanach, and The New Testament. The Christians' stands are that The Book of Mormon is not God inspired, creates three Gods out of the father, son, and holy ghost, and that Joseph Smith was a con man, along with many other faults found within the book."

"The Book of Mormon is no more valid than The Tanach and The New Testament. The Book of Mormon is all myth and has no more truth than the others. All of these books and the companion books such as The Apocrypha, The Talmud, and Doctrines and Covenants are the works of men. It is that, because of recent history, we know that Joseph Smith generated The Book of Mormon and its companion volumes through seer stones taken from the faked language of reformed Egyptian. Smith had the church purchase an Egyptian papyri that came though his Zion with a traveling museum. He interpreted it to be the word of God with revelations. Of course, Smith was the only one that could read it as it was in reformed Egyptian. Decades later, the papyri, was found to be the recordings of nothing more than the lives and deaths of Egyptian Gods. This fake, this con artist, is the first prophet of the LDS Church. So, why are there 15 million Mormon believers having faith in The Book of Mormon, The Book of Commandments, The Doctrine and Covenants, and

Pearl of Great Price? All of them are impossible to defend with any common sense, and a rudimentary understanding of anthropology, geology, archaeology, and history of the Americas, along with DNA research. And, to top it off, some of the DNA research was conducted at Brigham Young University, Provo, Utah."

"A little bit, no, a lot of bigotry. Mormons preferred their members to be white and delightsome. That is why the church was to run into legal problems in the latter part of the twentieth century. Think about it, have you ever met a Mormon of color? If you have it would be a distinct rarity."

"Come to think of it, I never have met a person of color that was a Mormon," replied Grace.

"Second Nephi 5:21, Smith had this transcribed about the Lamanites, '... *wherefore as they were white, and exceedingly fair and delightsome, that they might not be enticing unto my people the Lord God did cause a skin of blackness to come upon them'."*

"What follows came out of the mouth of Spencer W. Kimball, future president, apostle, seer, and prophet of the LDS Church, speaking at the 1960 LDS semi-annual conference, 'The work is unfolding, and blinded eyes begin to see, and scattered people begin to gather. I saw a striking contrast in the progress of the Indian people of today as of that of only 15 years ago. Truly, the scales of darkness are falling from their eyes, they are fast becoming a white and delightsome people. The day of the Lamanites is nigh. For years, they have been growing delightsome, and they are now becoming white and delightsome, as they were promised. In this picture of the 20 Lamanite missionaries, 15 of the 20 as light as Anglos, five were darker but equally as delightsome'."

"Kimball continues, 'The children in the home placement program in Utah are often lighter than their brothers and sisters in the hogans on the reservation. At one meeting, a father and mother with their 16 year old daughter was sitting between the dark father and mother, and it was evident she was several shades lighter than her parents; on the same reservation, in the same hogan, subject to the same sun and wind and weather. These young members of the Church are changing to whiteness and delightsomeness'," ended Zeus.

"And, from Second Nephi 1:23, *'And cursed shall be the seed of him that mixeth with their seed; for they shall be cursed even with the same cursing. And the Lord spake it, and it was done'.* This verse is referring *to* the inter-marrying of the Lamanites and the white, exceedingly fair, and delightsome Nephites," said Zeus.

"Let's talk about the ...ites," said Zeus.

"Huh?' asked Grace.

"The Lamanites and the Nephites," said Zeus.

"I wish you would," replied Grace.

"This is from the First Book of Nephi. The Book begins with an introduction, *'An account of Lehi and his wife Sariah, and his four sons, being called, beginning at the eldest, Laman, Lemuel, Sam, and Nephi. The Lord warns Lehi to depart out of the land of Jerusalem, because he prophesieth unto the people concerning their inquiry and they seek to*

145

destroy his life. He taketh three days' journey into the wilderness with his family. Nephi taketh his brethren and returneth to the land of Jerusalem after the record of the Jews. The account of their suffering. They take the daughters of Ishmael to wife. They take their families and depart into the wilderness. Their sufferings and their afflictions in the wilderness. The course of their travels. They come to the large waters. Nephi's brothers rebel against him. He confoundeth them, and buildeth a ship. They call the name of the place Bountiful. They cross the large waters into the promised land, and so forth. This is according to the account of Nephi; or in other words, I, Nephi, wrote this record'."

"And, from the Second Book of Nephi," Zeus began. "It reads, '*An account of the death of Nephi. Nephi's brothers rebel against him'*. The Lord warns Nephi to depart into the wilderness, and so forth."

"This all happens around 600 BC. Of note is the way that Smith diverts from The King James English to common language, such as '*in other words'* and '*so forth'*. Smith also uses the word '*nevertheless,* and in Second Nephi 4:28 transcribes, '*No longer droop in sin'*, but let's get back to the ...ites."

"As short as I can make it, here is the story. The family of Nephi; and the family of Ishmael get in a boat and come across the Atlantic to the promised land. Supposedly, they land on the shores of Panama. So, get this, Ishmael, the progenitor of Islam, is now in Central America."

"Oy vay," said Grace.

"Oy vay, is right," replied Zeus. "Let's go on. The brothers, Nephi and Laman, don't get along and soon Laman's people, the Lamanites, are punished with dark skin as they are filthy, and loathsome, and the dark scales will not drop from their eyes, according to God. It seems they fall out of favor with God and became apostates; those who have left the revealed-religion."

"On and off, Nephi's people, the Nephites, are in the favor of God or not, but in this case, God keeps them white and delightsome. Both the Lamanites and the Nephite spend a lot of their time wondering in the wilderness. This all happens over the centuries, and eventually, they clash in a huge battle around 385 BC, and the Lamanites wipe-out the Nephites; that is, they wipe-out all but one, a Nephite called Moroni, who later becomes an angel. Thus, North, Central, and South America are populated with the dark-skinned peoples now known as American Indians or Native Americans."

"You got all this stuff?" asked Zeus.

"I'm doing my best," replied Grace.

"Why don't we call it a night. We will continue with more ...ites tomorrow night. I realize this was a little much for one night," said Zeus.

"Oh no, I'll remember it. So, it's goodbye?" asked Grace.

"Yep, Bye."

"Bye," said Grace.

CHAPTER FOURTEEN

CELESTIAL, TERRESTRIAL, AND TELESTIAL

"Now to the Jaredites," said Zeus.

"Whoa, hang on a minute. Let me get my head on straight. Good evening, Zeus," said Grace.

"Good evening my dear Grace. Are you ready?" asked Zeus.

"I am. I have never heard of Lamanites, Nephites, and Jaredites," said Grace.

"Why this story of Jared, the progenitor of Noah, Noah's brother, and their followers was written about is hard to discern. All it does is give a substantial amount of truth that they didn't exist at all," began Zeus.

"He, Jared, and his brother lived in the time of the Tower of Babel. As the tale goes, they build ships, actually barges, and come across the Atlantic and settle, perhaps what is now known as Niagara Falls, New York. But, it is also described that they landed on a narrow neck of land in Central America. This is all in The Book of Ether; Ether, not Esther, in The Book of Mormon. They are said to have brought elephants with them. More about that later. The Jaredites form a kingdom, are wiped-out and never heard from again."

"That's it," asked Grace.

"That's it. They are thrown into Ether, it seems, for no reason at all," replied Zeus.

"Then, came the Mulekites who integrated with the Nephites."

"The Mulekites crossed the ocean and came to Central America. They are said to have harkened to the voice of the Lord. Mule was the last surviving son of Zedekiah when Babylon destroyed Jerusalem. They too, crossed the Atlantic and came upon the Nephites. But, the Mulekites could not be understood by the Nephites and the Nephites took them in and taught them their language, which I guess by then was not Hebrew. They established a new capitol, Zarahemla, and named the Nephite Mosiah as their king. It is also written that temples were built throughout the Americas."

"No towns or temples were ever found by the science of archaeology searching for the remains. Nothing of the remains of these people have ever been discovered; no ancient cities, no temples, nothing."

"All of the ...ites supposedly rode horses, but horses became extinct in the Americas between 8,000 and 12,000 years ago. However, horses were introduced in the Americas when the Spanish arrived in the 16th century AD."

Zeus continued. "And about those elephants of the Jaredites. No carcasses of elephants have ever been found in the Americas. However, fossils of mammoths have been found in the Americas, but mammoths became extinct 3,600 years ago."

"History shows that of the 900 languages of these supposed ancestors of the Lamanites, none is related to Hebrew at all."

"DNA evidence shows that 99.4% of Native Americans are of East Asian or Siberian descent, with the other .6% coming from the continent of Africa."

"No evidence at all?" asked Grace.

"None. Not one bit, it was all just made-up by Joseph Smith Junior," replied Zeus.

"Incredible," said Grace.

"Indeed, but get load of this," said Zeus.

"More supposed stuff?" asked Grace.

"Nope, this 'stuff' is for real, if you can call it reality," replied Zeus.

"I'm listenin'," said Grace.

"President, apostle, seer, prophet, revelator, and the very voice of scripture. The hierarchy of the LDS Church is not very complicated, but it is remarkable in its assumption that anyone in their right mind would believe it."

Zeus continued. "At the top there is the president. He, and it is always a he, is chosen by the fact that he is the longest serving apostle of the Quorum of 12 Apostles. Of course, this quorum is always white men. The president is not only the head of the church and an apostle, but is also dubbed a prophet, seer, and revelator."

"Below the president is the first counselor in the first presidency, followed by the second counselor, and then comes the president of the Quorum of Apostles. So, there are 15 apostles and they all have had a revelation from

God and a personal encounter with Jesus. One revelation was in 1965 when all 15 of them had the revelation that people of color could join the LDS Church. This was coincidental with the enactment of the Civil Rights Act because if the LDS Church did not admit people of color the church would have lost its tax-exempt status. A similar revelation occurred to all 15 of the apostles in 1978 when they had the revelation that people of color could enter the priesthood; coincidental with the filing of lawsuits against the church. These were powerful revelations to the apostles, white men, and hypocrites all."

"I must talk to one of these prophets," said Grace.

"What for?" asked Zeus.

"I want to see what is in the future for my investment portfolio," replied Grace.

"That is as good a reason as any," laughed Zeus.

"Or maybe I can see when I am going to get sprung from this joint," said Grace.

"Ah, but my dear, you will get sprung when we are finished," replied Zeus.

"When will that be?" asked Grace.

"Talk to one of the prophets," replied Zeus.

"I'll get right on it. Where are we going next?" asked Grace.

"To heaven," replied Zeus.

"There is no such place," said Grace.

"So, you are coming right along," began Zeus. "There are three kingdoms, one of lesser atonement, and an eternal sentence a Mormon will go upon death. Three are good places to go and one not so much; not so pleasant. There is the celestial kingdom where those that have lived a righteous life, accepted the teachings of Christ, lived up to all of the covenants of the LDS Church are bound for. The celestial resident will be given a white seer stone that will become Urim and Thummim; sound familiar. This is the kingdom of the sun."

"Then, there is the terrestrial kingdom where those who have lived a bit less than a righteous life will go. This is the kingdom of the moon."

"Ah, then there is the telestial kingdom."

"Telestial?" asked Grace.

"The word telestial was made up by Joseph Smith. This is where the dead in life, have lied, been a sorcerer, been an adulterer, and frequented the ladies of the night. These folks go first to a spirit prison where the inhabitants will suffer for one thousand years. Until the second coming, supposedly. Those adults who have lived from the day of Adam will go here until they accept the tenets of Mormonism. The telestial kingdom is the kingdom of the stars and will take in those that have completed their thousand years in spirit prison."

"Those that are eight or under, go directly to the celestial kingdom. Essentially, that would mean that there are no post-eight-year-olds in either the celestial or the terrestrial kingdoms as no one is all that perfect.

So, it begs the question, why do Mormons have those two kingdoms. The rest of the miscreants, well, they will reside with Lucifer for a long, long time."

"Smith may have been told about the works of Emmanuel Swedenborg. Someone had to tell him, as there is no proof of Smith being able to read. Anyway, Swedenborg wrote that there are three heavens, each distinct from the other. Swedenborg called the highest level of heaven celestial, and that the heavens correspond to the sun, the moon, and the stars. Swedenborg never mentioned a terrestrial and a telestial heaven."

"Now, if you were really a 'don't bee', instead of a 'do bee', and said a lot of 'my bads', you end up with Satan in perdition; a state of eternal punishment and damnation into which a sinful person passes after death. It must be a resentment thing."

"Somehow, after the Adam and Eve fallen bit, for no explained reason, some do end-up in the celestial kingdom where the men enjoy constant sex with unlimited women and those women are constantly pregnant, so they can give birth to little spirits that come to Earth, enter the womb of women who give birth to little Mormons. Really, Smith had those things transcribed."

"Also, it reads that each man and woman in the celestial kingdom will become a god with their own planet to oversee. But, with constant sex, and constant spirit births, how do they have the time?" reflected Zeus.

"Supposedly, the God of the LDS Church was once a mortal man just as are the celestial inhabitants. That means that God, as a person, came down from heaven, had sex with Mary, who was betrothed to Joseph, and from that union Jesus was born. Thus, according Mormonism, Jesus was not born of a virgin as the New Testament proports. This was transcribed from Joseph Smith reading the seer stones.

"This is all in those four books?" asked Grace.

"Yes, indeed," replied Zeus. "You like potpourri, don't you?"

"You bet. This ought to be good," replied Grace.

"Okay, potpourri," began Zeus. "it is also written that Jesus Christ visited the Americas in 34 AD, after his resurrection."

"Smith foretold that the coming of Christ would be in 1891. A false prophet indeed."

"In The Book of Abraham in The Pearl of Great Price the planet Kolob is nearest to the throne of God. No planet Kolob has been found nor named such by any astronomers."

"God sits on God's throne and rests his feet on the Earth."

"Smith and Brigham Young taught that there are inhabitants on the moon and the sun."

"Jesus is really the brother of Lucifer in the spirit world."

"There is no archaeological evidence to support Mormonism, that is why there are no maps in any Mormon literature."

"The angel Michael came down to Earth as Adam."

"The angel Gabriel came to Earth as Noah."

'In the Third Book of Nephi, 20:19 it reads, '... *thou shalt beat in pieces many people'*."

"In the Third Book of Nephi 21:18 it reads, '... *so I will destroy the cities'*."

"In Moroni 10:6 it reads, '... *nothing that is good denieth the Christ'*."

"Of course, that is the Mormon Christ. So, we take from that quote, that all but 15,000,000 Mormons on this Earth are unworthy."

"Latter-day Saints, apostles, prophets, seers, and revelators, to whom God reveals all sorts of things, thus, we can see why so many have become the flock. Maybe that is unfair, as the children didn't volunteer for Mormonism and they are in the count. Utah is 75% Mormon and that state has a higher than national average rate of child abuse, incest, divorce, suicides, spousal abuse, and bankruptcies."

"Here are some interesting facts about Mormonism, some of which are not found in other Christian religions."

"Mormons do not display a crucifix."

"The age of eight is considered the age of accountability."

"Young women in Bible study are broken into three groups; 12 and 13, beehives; 14 and 15, Mia Maids; and 16 and above, Laurels."

"When the prophet, the president of the church speaks, it is scripture."

"Good grief," said Grace.

"Exactly," replied Zeus. "Children born of single mothers are to be put up for adoption so they can live in a 'proper home'."

"A couples first kiss should be on the marriage alter."

"The bishop decides punishment for sins. Which seems to me would be completely subjective."

"Mormons, supposedly, live longer than those not in the fold."

"Tithes are mailed to the bishop."

"The LDS Church does not disclose financial information."

"The LDS Church took a stand 'against' the Equal Rights Amendment in the 1970s."

"Mormons consider spirit to be matter."

"To Mormons, God looks like a man."

"Lucifer is one of God's oldest spirit children."

"The LDS Church expects to build a New Jerusalem in Missouri before the second coming of Christ."

"Mormons spoke in tongues in the early days of the church."

"All Mormons can receive revelations, but only about their own lives."

"Mormons reject the Christian idea of the universe being created out of nothing."

"All Mormons have a pre-mortal life in celestial heaven."

"Free will is referred to as agency or free agency."

"Mormons reject the idea of original sin."

"The celestial kingdom is reserved for married couples only."

"The LDS Church is the 'only true and living church'."

"Latter-day is used to describe the end times being near."

"Priesthood ordinances include 'healing' the sick."

"A 'healing blessing' can save a Mormon's life unless God wills differently."

"I'm sorry, but that is absolute nonsense," said Grace

"The LDS Church is totally patriarchal."

"Mormons baptize the dead; including Jews. They have baptized over 100 million deceased persons. Jews find exception to this practice. No good explanation has ever been found for this practice."

The president apostle, seer, revelator, and prophet rules. The LDS Church is not a democracy."

"Joseph Smith received a divine revelation to transcribe a new version of The King James Bible."

"As with Christian fundamentalists, Mormons believe humans have inhabited the Earth for only six thousand years."

"Joseph Smith said, 'It is a shame for women to rule in the church'."

"Thomas S. Monson, the sixteenth president of the LDS Church said, 'Every good woman knows the back hand'."

"What?" said Grace.

"Yes, the sixteenth president, apostle, seer, revelator, and prophet, Thomas S. Monson, was a wife beater," said Zeus. "And that brings us to tomorrow night's talk."

"Give me a hint," said Grace.

"Let's call tomorrow night, 'And then there was Lilith'," replied Zeus.

"Sounds interesting. I won't ask anymore. Is this goodnight?" asked Grace.

"I think you have had enough over the last two nights. Don't you?" replied Zeus.

"I have. It's Bye then?"

"Bye."

CHAPTER FIFTEEEN

TWO WOMEN FOR ONE MAN

"Hello."

"Hello."

"Tonight, let's start at the beginning. Let's start with Genesis," said Zeus.

"A good place to start," said Grace.

"It's been years, ago, but do you remember when you first learned the story of Adam and Eve?" asked Zeus.

"Of course, I can. I don't remember how old I was, but I do remember this story as being one of the very first stories I learned in Sunday school. It is the start of the Bible, where we learned what day God created certain things on the earth. If I remember correctly, God made Adam and Eve on the sixth day before creating the Sabbath on the seventh day. I remember, too, thinking how strange it was that God took a rib from Adam and created Eve. And although I learned about God making them leave the Garden of Eden after they both ate some forbidden fruit, I didn't really understand why." Replied Grace

"Yes, now that you know the story, you know God's reason. But, as a child, understandably, the story doesn't have any real meaning. A bigger question for you, though, do you know the other version of the story?" asked Zeus.

"No, not really. I just thought the story was written differently in other verses," replied Grace.

"Most people do think it is just one story. But, there is much more to the story. Some scholars suggest there are at least two versions. So, let's revisit Genesis. In Genesis 1:27, it reads, '*So God created man in His own image, in the image God created him; male and female He created them*'. There are some things to point out in this verse. You can't really tell by the words who God created first. Was it man or was it woman? Maybe that was the intent. Also, although you know the story with Adam and Eve, the names aren't mentioned in the first chapter of Genesis version," said Zeus.

"Interesting. I hadn't really thought of either of the things you just pointed out. Continue," replied Grace.

"Maybe an even more interesting bit of information about this verse of Genesis is that some consider this woman to be the first woman, the first wife God created for man. She is referred to as Lilith, who is brought up later in The Tanach, not the Christian Old Testament," said Zeus.

"Oh, yes, I have heard of Lilith, but from what I remember, Lilith was often envisioned as a dangerous demon of the night, who is sexually wanton, and who steals babies in the darkness. I assume Lilith was linked in part to a historically earlier class of female demons in certain ancient religions," said Grace.

"That is correct. But, more importantly to this story, Lilith would not succumb to the inferior position or even sleep with Adam and flies away from the Garden of Eden. When God sends three angles to ask her to come back, but she refuses and is disobedient to God, God turns her into a monster or demon. So, the story goes, she copulated with demons, conceiving hundreds more. She turned into being the woman you remembered," said Zeus.

"I don't recall this being Adam's first woman or even learning there was more than one woman, that God created for Adam. There is what I thought a repeat of this story in the second chapter of Genesis but didn't realize it was a different version. If this the interpretation, that Adam had two wives, it would certainly be understood why the churches, the religions wouldn't explain this difference. A woman leaving a man? A split-up and in the first chapter of the Bible? I suppose you could call it the creation of the first divorce. Not funny. I suppose there isn't any religion that discusses this version," said Grace.

"How true. But, if one really studies the different books of the different religions, the Lilith story is not original as with the preponderance of tales told in The Tanach, the Christian Old Testament, The New Testament, and The Book of Mormon. Here's another interesting bit about Lilith. Where she is mentioned in the Bible in The Book of Isaiah of the Christian Old Testament, she still is not mentioned by name. Isaiah 34:14 reads, *'The*

161

creatures of the desert will meet with wolves, a goat will cry out; and there the night monster will be and find a place to rest'," said Zeus.

"Even that seems a stretch to have this person to be known as Lilith," said Grace.

"Although Lilith is not actually identified by name except for Isaiah in The Tanach, Isaiah 34:14 which reads, 'Martens encounter cats, and the satyrs call out to each other; then Lilith will rest and find relaxation', this probably provides the reasoning why The Tanach version calls her Lilith, with the words almost identical in both books," said Zeus.

"Yes, that makes sense, now," said Grace.

"Let us continue, then. With Lilith out of the picture and God, wanting Adam to have a woman, He created a second wife for him. That's who we know as Eve. And to catch you off guard, even in the second Biblical story of Adam and Eve, the better-known creation story of man and woman, they are not named. They remain simply man and woman. This creation story is in Genesis 2: 21 – 23 and reads, ' *...So the LORD God caused the man to fall into a sleep, and while he slept, He took one of the man's ribs and closed up the area with flesh. And from the rib that the God had taken from man, He made a woman and brought her to him. And the man said: "This is now bone of my bones and flesh of my flesh; she shall be called 'woman,' for out of man she was taken,"* said Zeus.

Is there any similarity in the Tanach to the Christian Bible version?

"Yes," replied Zeus. "The Tanach, Genesis 2:21-23, reads almost identical. *'So, Hashem God cast a deep sleep upon the man, and Hashem God took from the man's side and healed flesh over it. Hashem God made the side into a woman. Hashem brought the woman to the man. This time it is my bone and flesh. Woman she will be called for she is of man'*. The main difference is that the word 'rib' is not used in the Tanach version."

"Even though, they are almost identical, but unlike the first woman that the man knew, both these versions seem to have a very different meaning to me on how God thought of woman... after the Lilith creation. With God creating Eve from the Adam's rib, this suggests that the woman is subordinate to man," said Grace.

"This could be an assumption of some truth, considering that women continue to be considered subservient, even to this day, in most religions. And although the time line of why God may have actually believed this, He does not let on any feeling one way or another about woman until Eve, this second wife, talks Adam into eating the fruit. First, tempted by the serpent to pluck it from the tree and then to eat it, when God learns that Eve tempted Adam, God shows how upset He is with the woman, Eve, not Adam," said Grace.

"And as the story goes, they were cast out of the Garden of Eden," said Grace.

"And even worse for the women, God sentenced Eve to be ruled by the man and worse, yet, He multiplied the pain of childbirth for the woman. Genesis 3:16 reads, *'I will greatly multiply your pain in childbirth,*

163

in pain you shall bring forth children; Yet your desire shall be for your husband, and he shall rule over you'," said Zeus.

"Even though Lilith would not return to the man as God had commanded, it never came to be that Adam would rule over Lilith as he rules over Eve," said Grace.

"Maybe because of the additional wrath from God towards the woman, considering the perceived position of the women in virtually all religions, this may be why this is the universally accepted story of God's creation of man and woman. This is the one you remember from Sunday school. But, I suspect, this was just a story to you. There is no way children could begin to understand the real reason God banned them from the Garden of Eden. When you think of it, it is even amazing that this became a childhood story to teach in Sunday schools. To talk of God being disobeyed seems contradictory for children. Regardless, there is more to this story that most have never heard. Ready?" asked Zeus.

Yes. Please, continue," said Grace.

"Unlike the two versions, where man and women are not given names in this version, of a myth, the man and woman are given names. The man who is called Enki in this story falls ill and feels a pain in his rib. Ninhursag of this story creates a goddess from this rib. Her name is called Ninti. Ninti in the Sumerian version means 'Lady of the Rib' or 'Lady of the Living'. This myth dates back even further than the story of the man and woman that is in The Tanach, but the similarities to the

Christian Old Testament and The Tanach versions are quite obvious," said Zeus.

"It sure appears that the Christian and Jewish story of the creation of man and woman may have originated from a myth, a much older myth. Enki and Ninti, Adam and Eve," said Grace.

"And that the story you learned from the Bible is similar should provide further questioning rather than confirmation of the stories appearing in the Christian Old Testament and Tanach as well as The Book of Mormon. Regardless of the timing or the wording, in all of the accounts, it is my suggestion that they be considered symbolic rather than scientific. If you can refer to any scripture as scientific," said Zeus.

"I agree. And to think all of these years, I have held onto my Sunday school version. As with so much of what I have learned from you, although all is enlightening, sometimes I am now feeling I have more questions than answers," said Grace.

"No need to worry," said Zeus. "If you continue this journey, you will eventually find your truth. I think we have had enough of the 'beginning' for this night. But, it may now provide additional insight as we discuss the plight of women in the scriptures...our next lesson together."

"I look forward to tomorrow night," said Grace.

"Good bye."

"Good night."

CHAPTER SIXTEEN

LADIES LAST

"Hello. How was your day?" asked Zeus.

"A little slow. You gave me a lot to think about last night," said Grace.

"Yes, I know... Tonight, we are going to talk about women's issues in The Tanach, The New Testament, and The Book of Mormon. The verses of The Tanach I will discuss is but a small sampling of the contempt towards women."

"Before I came here, when I started questioning my faith, I picked up a book by Christopher Hitchens; 'god is not Great'. In the title, God is in lower case. One quote stuck with me. Hitchens wrote, 'The holy book in the longest continuous use, The Talmud, commands the observant one to thank his maker that he was not born a woman'," said Grace.

"If one follows biblical text, that is true. I've wondered if women took the time to read the Bible, would they so blindly continue to be a member of a revealed-religion," said Zeus.

"I am ready for the truth," said Grace.

"Good," replied Zeus. Let's get started with Genesis 4:19, '*Lamesh took to himself two wives ... ',"*

"Genesis 16:7-9, '*She was found by a spring in the desert. It was at the spring on the path to Shur when the angel said, 'Hagar where have you been*

and you are on your way to what place?' Hagar said, 'I am going far away from my mistress, Sarai'. The angel of Hashem God said to Hagar, 'Return to your mistress Sarai, and submit to her domination of you'."

"Genesis 21:10, 'Out goes this slave Hagar with her son. That son of my husband born from her will not get one piece of silver, nothing goes to him, it goes to our son Isaac'."

"So, the son of Hagar and Abraham, Ishmael, will get no inheritance? It all goes to Isaac?" asked Grace.

"Correct. Now listen to this one," replied Zeus. "Exodus 22:17, 'You will not allow a sorceress to live'. What's the purpose of making a woman a sorceress? How demeaning."

"Leviticus 18:19, 'A woman who is unclean will not be approached'. Who determines if a woman is unclean? What does unclean mean"

"Leviticus 19:20, 'If a man lies down with a slave woman, but she is to be the property of another man and the woman is not redeemed and she is not to be freed; it will be investigated. The slave woman will not be killed because she is not free'."

"Leviticus 20:10, 'If a man and a woman commit adultery, both the man and the woman will be killed'. Just listen to what I am quoting. It all degrades women and the men they are with."

"Leviticus 20:27, 'If a man or woman practices sorcery of Yid'oni or Ov, the man or woman will be killed by stoning'."

"How cruel. They sin together, and they must die. What about forgiveness?" asked Grace.

"Now to Leviticus 21:19, *'A Kohan's daughter will not commit adultery, it will shame her father. She must be consumed by fire'.*"

"When they took a census of the children of Israel, with their families, *'every male will be counted'*, but, there is nothing said about counting the females."

"God does not like females in this next one either, at least not women who have 'known' a man. Instead, the next reading sounds as if it is encouraging grown men to 'go after' little girls. Today if you read this in the newspapers, the men would be labeled as pedophiles. And, as if this is not sick enough, the women are killed to justify the men taking children," said Zeus.

"Numbers 1:2, *'Kill all of the male children and kill every woman who has known a man you will kill. But the young children who have not known a man, you will let them live and you may keep them for yourselves'.*"

"In this next one, it sounds as if everyone is killed; men, women, and children. In Deuteronomy 20:13-15 it reads, *'Hashem God will deliver the males to be killed with a sword. You may plunder all that is in the city; the children, the women, and the livestock, as all in the city is booty. You will possess the booty for yourselves for Hashem God gave it to you'.*"

"Just one chapter later, the beautiful women become the spoils of war. In Deuteronomy 21:10-11 it reads, *'When you go to war in the name of Hashem God you may capture all, but the women beautiful in form, that you desire, you may have and marry'.* This makes no sense when all other chapters find fault with women with horrific ways to punish them."

"In the next chapter, Deuteronomy 22:20-21, *'If it is a fact that the signs of virginity were not to be found in the girl, she will be delivered to the house of her father and there she will be stoned to death. For the evil and the outrage against Israel will be removed for she has brought shame on her father's house'.* Now, pray-tell. How does a father know if his daughter is a virgin? And, making this passage even more sick, it approves of killing the female child. What about the man who took her virginity?"

"Ah, again a woman has to be a virgin ... or die," said Zeus. "In the next one the father gets paid if his daughter sins. What again, happens to the man who slept with her."

"Deuteronomy 22:28-29, *'If a man lies with a young girl who is not betrothed and it is found out the man will pay the father fifty pieces of silver. They will be married and they cannot divorce'.*"

"Chattel, just plain chattel," said Grace.

"And it continues ... and ... gets worse. Zechariah 14:1-2, *'The day is coming for Hashem God when the spoils of war will be divided. All the nations of Jerusalem will be gathered to capture the city. Then the city will be pillaged and the women will be violated '.*"

"Listen to this. This is so wrong. It basically says it is alright to rape women. These readings from The Tanach ... well ... appalling, is not a strong enough word and the despicable things that The Tanach allows to be done to women. And, all of this denigration of women is done in the name of Hashem God. Grace, this is the god you loved. The god you preached about."

"Thus, ends our look into The Tanach. Appalling is not a strong enough word for it. Disgusting, to say the least. So much of the denigration of women is done in the name of Hashem God. But we are not finished by a long shot. There is more to come in The New Testament."

"No, this is not the god I thought I knew and loved," said Grace.

"And, all of this is in the Old Testament, to lie dormant for all time. You were taught what the religious scholars wanted you to know. They cherry picked the topics for you. You probably read this, but you never had any professor teach you any of it? Right??" asked Zeus.

"Yes, you are right. I never heard any of this discussed while going to seminary. But, what bothers me more is that I don't even remember reading this in The Old Testament." replied Grace.

"It is not totally your fault. You have been taught and learned the lesson well. And, that is, to only look at the good stuff. The ten commandments, ... well ... you were interested in those. But, the Battle of Jericho, you just read past it, as it was not what you were looking for," replied Zeus.

"And, The New Testament. Is it the same as far as women are concerned?" asked Grace.

"Let's just say, the feminist agenda in The New Testament is not the definition with which you are familiar. There is nothing in this either that has anything to do with equal rights for women. Quite the opposite, it is about a socialist, anti-family political movement that encourages women to leave their husbands, kill their children, practice witchcraft, destroy capitalism and become lesbians," said Zeus.

"I certainly didn't remember … well … it to be all of that," said Grace.

"No, you wouldn't. This is a quote from a Southern Baptist who doesn't deserve the high regards his followers bestow upon him," said Zeus.

"The holiness of God is not evidenced in women when they are brash, brassy, boisterous, head-strong, strong-willed, loud-mouthed, over-talkative, having to have the last word, challenging, controlling, manipulative, critical, conceited, arrogant, aggressive, assertive, strident, interruptive, undisciplined, insubordinate, disruptive, dominating, domineering, or clamoring for power. Rather, women accept God's holy order and character by being humbly and unobtrusively respectful, and functional subordination to God, church leadership, and husbands."

"Oh, that has to be from a televangelist," replied Grace.

"That's right. It is a quote by James Fowler, a Professor of Theology at Emory University, a school that teaches creationism as science. It must have been very hard on the female students in his classes that had to listen to him. One wonders how many women were in his classes," replied Zeus. "Listen to this, another demeaning comment about women. 'Men have broad and large chests, and small narrow hips, and more understanding then women, who have but small and narrow breasts, and broad hips, to the end they should remain at home, sit still, keep house, and bear and bring up children'. That is from Martin Luther," said Zeus.

"The leader of the Lutheran Church. I had no idea so many church leaders had such horrid things to say about women," replied Grace.

"See if you recognize who might have said this. 'Thus, the women, who have perversely exceeded her proper bounds, is forced back to her own position. She, had indeed, previously been subject to her husband, but that was liberal and gentle subjection; now, however, she is cast into servitude'," said Zeus.

"John Calvin," said Grace. "I do remember reading that some time ago. I couldn't understand how the Calvinists, in addition to being anti-woman, believed in predestination from conception. What's the point of living if one is predestined from conception to go to heaven or hell? There is nothing the congregant can do about it, either. It cries out for two questions: Who decides what the predestination is for the church member? And, greater yet, why go to church?"

"To the first question; elders of the church. And to the second question. Good point," said Zeus. "Here is another from a man considered equally as great to have a university named after him. He saw his flock a little differently – insignificant. 'Do not any longer contend for mastery, for power, money, or praise. Be content to be a private, insignificant person, known and loved by God and me ... of what importance is your character to mankind, if you were buried just now. Or if you had ever lived, what loss would I be to the cause of God'?"

'That's what John Wesley wrote in a letter to his wife. And to think, of all the people who followed these men," said Zeus.

"It does make one speculate as to why they followed them," replied Grace.

"Here's two more. This is from Tertullian around 155 to 240 AD, 'Woman is a temple built over a sewer'. And, from Saint Clement of Alexandria, speaking about women, 'the very consciousness of their nature must evoke feelings of shame'. These are words from a saint," said Zeus.

"Now, back to The New Testament, Matthew 19:29, *'And everyone who has left houses or brothers or sisters or father or mother or children or farms for My names sake, will garner that which is plenty and will abide in heaven forever'*. Okay, just drop everything, abandon your children and go preach for God. Not very family oriented."

"In this next reading, the ladies place in the scriptures is contradictory to other scripture readings. There is no apparent reason as to what makes her so special," asked Zeus.

"Who are you talking about?" asked Grace.

"She is in Acts of the Apostles 9:36-42, *'Now in Joppa there was a disciple named Dorcus of the Greeks, but Tabitha in Hebrew. Tabitha was full of kindness and she was charitable. Tabitha became sick and died. After her body was washed she was taken to the upper room. Lydda is near Joppa, and they heard that Peter was there, men went to say to Peter, 'Do not delay. Come with us'. Peter followed them to Joppa. The widows were crying over the body of Tabitha as Peter was brought into the room. They wore the clothes that Tabitha made when she was alive. Peter asked them to leave and then he began praying over the body. Peter said, 'Arise'. She opened her eyes and sat up in the presence of Peter. He presented her alive to the people of Joppa, and thus many believed in the Lord'.* There are those in the clergy that preach that Tabitha the 13th disciple of Jesus Christ but does not say. Did you ever tell this story in a sermon?" asked Zeus.

"No. I have never preached about Tabitha. I never thought of her as a 13th disciple," replied Grace.

"Tabitha, you have to admit, was a rarity. For the most part, women are considered lower than low," replied Zeus.

"And then, there are these next passages. How do you make this work in 2018? But, the passages may provide an explanation as to why nuns wore habits. Let's go to First Corinthians 13:34-35, *'Women are not permitted to speak in the church. They are to subject themselves, and the Law says. To learn of the scriptures, they must ask their husbands at home, not speak in church',"* quoted Zeus.

"Colossians 3:18, *'The Lord demands that wives be compliant in the company of their husbands'."*

"This next passage gives credence to some religions to not even allow women in the hierarchy of the church. First Timothy 2:9-15, *'Women must wear proper clothing. Women must be modest and discreet. They may not braid their hair nor wear jewelry for this is how they make a claim of Godliness. Women must submit to biblical instruction. Women must be quiet and never be given authority over a man. Adam was created before Eve. It was not Adam who was first deceived by the serpent. It was Eve who transgressed. For that women will be in great pain bearing children. They are to show love of their husbands by showing self-restraint'.* This is

174

all because Adam was deceived, but he wasn't, he just took a bite of the fruit. And, for that bite, women will have painful births." said Zeus.

"What a horrible, spiteful thing, with which to condemn women," replied Grace.

"But, at least in this case, it is not God speaking. This is from Paul. He took authority much as Joseph Smith does later on, as we will discuss'," said Zeus. "Now onto The Book of Mormon."

"Please, continue," said Grace.

"No surprise, with what was written in The New Testament books that The Book of Mormon dictates the submission of women," began Zeus. "In The Book of Mormon women are made out to be harlots, objects of the Lord as the Lord looks at their private parts. According to Mormonism, women are filthy and deserving of burning, unclean and to be avoided; of course, they are witches. What I am going to talk about is but a sampling of the writings of the misogynists that created The Book of Mormon. Didn't have much good to say about women ... but wait."

"First Nephi 13:6-8, as transcribed from the ramblings of Joseph Smith. *'And it came to pass ...*

"Another, 'and it came to pass. Unbelievable. Sorry, please continue," said Grace.

"That's okay. *'And it came to pass that I beheld this great and abominable church; and I saw the devil that he was the founder of it. And I also saw gold, and silver, and silks, and scarlets, and fine twined linen, and the precious clothing, and I saw many harlots. And the angel spake unto me,*

175

saying: *'Behold the gold, and the silver, and the silks, and the scarlets, and the fine twined linen, and the precious clothing, and the harlots, are the desires of this great and abominable church'.* Oh, but, there is more," said Zeus.

"Again, from The Book of Mormon, Second Nephi 13:16-17, *'Moreover the Lord saith: Because the daughters of Zion are haughty, and walk with stretched-forth necks, and wanton eyes, walking and mincing as they go, and making a twinkling with their feet – Therefore the Lord will smite with a scab the crown of the head of the daughters of Zion, and the Lord will discover their secret parts'.* The Zion mentioned here is the one in Missouri. 'With a scab the crown of the head' must be psoriasis. And I must ask, again, why does God have such a preoccupation with the birth canal?" said Zeus.

"We are still discussing Missouri, and in The Book of Mormon, Second Nephi 14:4. *"When the Lord shall have washed away the filth of the daughters of Zion and shall have purged the blood of Jerusalem from the midst thereof by the spirit of judgement and by the spirit of burning'.* Smith goes all the way from Missouri to Palestine or maybe Ohio or maybe Indiana or maybe Illinois with the filth and the blood."

"And then, Third Nephi 20:14, *'And then shall a cry go forth: Depart ye, depart, go ye out from thence, touch that which is not unclean; go ye out of the midst of her; be ye clean, that bear the vessels of the Lord.*"

"It's amazing when you think about it … Why would any woman even want to be with a man who thinks so little of her? I wonder if women had written those books would they have written such horrid things about men? I don't think women were any different in those days compared to now. So, it is hard to conceive women to think such cruelty towards men," said Grace.

"Third Nephi 21:16,19, *'And I will cut off witchcrafts out of thy land, and thou shalt have no more soothsayers. And it shall come to pass that all lying, and deceivings, and envyings, and strifes, and priestcrafts, and whoredoms, shall be done away'*. It sounds like all women, even in the LDS Church are seen as harlots or in whoredoms. According to The Book of Mormon, it states that all Roman Catholic women would be prostitutes. Why just the Catholics?" asked Zeus. "It makes no sense."

"I feel sorry for the women born into this religion. How can they ever escape such male dominance?" When you hear it read aloud, it is hard to believe anyone would want anything to do with this religion. Smith's attitude towards women ... well ... it is shameful," said Grace.

"And yet, today, look how the church flourishes," replied Zeus.

"Ether 10:5, *'And it came to pass,'* Once again with the 'It came to pass'. *That Riplakish did not do that which is right in the sight of the Lord, for he did have many wives and concubines'*. What we have here is Smith dictating for transcription that polygamy is not right in the sight of the Lord. Smith painted himself into a corner with this one verse with a huge contradiction. Smith and Brigham Young had as many as 40 wives. This is a quote from a CNN documentary, 'The founder of the Mormon Church, Joseph Smith, wed as many as 40 wives, including some who were already married and one as young as 14 years old, the church acknowledged in a surprising new essay. Smith's marital history had been the subject of frequent historical debate, but until recently, Mormon leaders had taken

177

pains to present its founding prophet as happily married to one woman. Now, the church says, 'careful estimates put the number between 30 and 40. The church, officially called the Church of Jesus Christ of Latter-day Saints, disavowed plural marriage in 1890 under pressure of the U.S. government, which had imprisoned polygamists and seized their assets'. But, even today, there are those that are polygamists in secret to avoid the government from getting involved. Then how about this," asked Zeus. "I think no more of taking a wife than buying a cow ... "

"I don't understand," said Grace.

"It is from the book 'Taking a Wife and Buying a Cow' by Ann-Eliza Snow, nee' Webb, the 19th wife of Brigham Young," replied Zeus.

"Okay. Why bring her up? What does the quote have anything to do with this," asked Grace.

"Let me start over," began Zeus. "I think no more of taking a wife than I do of buying a cow, was one of Heber Kimball's delicate remarks, made from the stand in the Tabernacle to the congregation of several thousand. Most of the hearers thought even less of it, for they would have to pay money for the cow; and as for the other, he had only to throw his handkerchief to some girl, and she would pick it up and follow him."

"How does a woman have any self-esteem in this religion? You don't hear anything about Mormon women, do you? The way they are thought about explains why." said Grace.

"Heber C. Kimball was one of the original 12 apostles in the Mormon church," said Zeus.

"Emma, Joseph Smith's wife, frequently denied that her husband had ever taken additional wives. But, it was a lie. Over the years that Emma was married to him, she had to deal with the humiliation of Smith having many wives. In April of 1841, Smith wed Louisa Beaman. During the next two and a half years, Smith married or was sealed to about 30 additional women, ten of whom were already married to other men. Some of the polyandrous marriages were done with the consent of the first husbands, and some plural marriages may have been considered, eternity only, sealings. Ten of Smith's wives were between the ages of 14 and 20; others were over 50. In 1843, Emma temporarily accepted Smiths marriage to four women boarded in the Smith household, but soon regretted her decision and demanded the other wives leave. It is amazing she waited so long to ask them to leave"

"In The Book of Mormon, where are the women? The Tanach, The Christian Old and New Testaments, mentions 188 unique women by name; in The Book of Mormon, only three women are mentioned from The Old and New Testaments; Eve, Sarah, and Mary. Another three were made-up by Smith; Sariah, Isabel, and Abish. They all play minor roles in The Book of Mormon.

"Mormon Doctrine 844, written by Bruce R. McConkie, a member of the Quorum of 12 Apostles from nineteen 1972 until 1985. I quote, 'The Mormon position on women has changed little since the early 1800s, when the official view was that, 'woman's primary place is in the home, where she is to rear children and abide by the righteous counsel of her husband'."

"Now, from an article in the June 1975 issue of Ensign magazine, '[Women], you are to become a career woman in the greatest career on Earth – that of homemaker, wife, and mother. It was never intended by the Lord that married women should compete with men in employment. They have a far greater and more important service to render'. That was in '75, as late as '75. In this day and age, it is amazing that any woman is a member of the Mormon church. It is their way of life. In a certain way the women have been brain- washed."

"How have they survived and lived like this all these years?" asked Grace. "The only way is for a woman to be totally submissive. It just seems so sad."

"It doesn't say. Again, from Ol' Heber Kimball, 'Women are to be led, counseled, and directed. And, If I am not a good man, I have no right in this Church to a wife or wives, or the power to propagate my species. What then should be done with me? Make a eunuch of me and stop my propagation'."

"I caught the 'wives' bit, said Grace.

"Apparently, some of the Mormon women did rebel in their own way against the teachings of the church. Get this. In an effort to control women of the Mormon church ... well ... listen. It's from Spencer W. Kimball, not to be mixed up with the late Heber. Spencer was the 12th president, apostle, seer, revelator, and prophet of the LDS Church. 'Too many mothers work away from home to furnish sweaters and music lessons and trips and fun for their children. Too many women spend their time in socializing, in politicking, in public services when they should be home to teach and train and receive and love their children into security'."

"When did this male chauvinist serve as president?" asked Grace.

"From 1973 to 1985," replied Zeus. "Ah, but there is more from Ol' Spencer. I quote from the book One Nation Under Gods: A History of the Mormon Church. Kimball advised the departing missionaries as follows: The brother missionaries have been in the habit of picking out the prettiest woman for themselves before they get here and bringing on the ugly ones for us; therefore, you have to bring them all here before taking any one of them and let us have a fair shake'."

"I can't begin to imagine having to live as the Mormon women have had to live all these years … even now. If I believed in hell, to me, the Mormon life would be hell on earth," said Grace. "No wonder they won't let anyone not of their religion in their temples. They know it is wrong and are afraid of any outside influence. It will continue to go on."

"You seem a little ticked," said Zeus.

"No, I'm more than ticked," replied Grace. "This type of brain-washing is despicable, and below disgraceful, that a religion is allowed to treat women this way. No better than a piece of furniture."

"I do wonder why the LDS Church allows women into Brigham Young University," began Zeus. "It is such a contradiction to the religion. I guess the school needs the tuition for its coffers. The Tanach, The Christian Old Testament, The New Testament do their fair share of demeaning women, but The Book of Mormon goes over the top in demeaning women. Equality of women in the church should not even be an issue in 2018. Even our constitution says all are equal. There is no excuse that this type of treatment is allowed to continue. Yet with the Mormon's present hierarchy so spelled out in The Book of Mormon. Unfortunately, I see little change for equality, any time soon, in the Mormon Church."

"I could not agree with you more," said Grace.

"And, there is more … so much more. But, you have had a lot to remember and think about these last two nights. So, tomorrow night will be a little lighter load," replied Zeus.

"I'm ready for a reprieve," said Grace. "I can't imagine there being more of these tyrannical beliefs. Is there?"

"You can decide upon my next visit," replied Zeus.

"Can you give me a hint?" asked grace.

"Let me cogitate a moment," replied Zeus. "Ah, let's call tomorrow night, 'thou shalt not suffer a witch to live'."

"We must be ready to talk about Catholicism? Right?" asked Grace.

"With an affirmative, now I'll say, until tomorrow."

"So, it's goodnight?" asked Grace.

"Don't miss your groups. Night," said Zeus.

"I won't. Bye," said Grace.

CHAPTER SEVENTEEN

INQUISITIONS," SAID THE POPE, "SORRY."

"Grace. Grace."

"Where have you been the last two nights?" asked Grace.

"I thought you might want a reprieve from so much wretchedness," laughed Zeus.

"Yes, it has been a lot to take in," replied Grace.

"Tonight, it will be easier on you. I have a little history that might surprise you. We are going to discuss, 'Thou shalt not suffer a witch to live'," said Zeus.

"Ah, witches. As in the Wiccans?" asked Grace.

"No, as with the Inquisition," replied Zeus. "First, though, before we get started, let me provide a definition of the word 'inquisition'. It is a period of prolonged and intensive questioning that in this instance is for the total suppression of heresy, as the Catholic Church defined heresy."

"Oh, please continue," said Grace.

"Okay, about the Inquisitions," Zeus began. "There were many of them. The Peruvian, Mexican, Portuguese, and Inquisitional courts held in their empire states in Africa, Asia, and the Americas, along with the Papal Inquisitions. However, the greatest amount and most horrid Inquisitions were held by the Spanish and their authority reached beyond their boundaries into France and Italy. Now, comes the reason that the Roman Catholic church would just as soon be left out of the history books."

"All of these Inquisitions were held with the permission of the Papacy and were conducted by the Cardinals, Archbishops, Bishops, and Priests on three continents. It's so difficult to believe they were men of the cloth? It is a period that I can understand the church not wanting to discuss." asked Zeus.

"That question is rhetorical, I take it," replied Grace

"The preponderance of the victims, those adjudged heretics and burned at the stake or left to rot in prison were women. And, then the witches were killed according to the authorities of the Roman Catholic Church who were in league with the local authorities."

"Simply put, Exodus 22:17, 'You shall not permit a sorceress to live'."

"That verse alone is the justification for the Inquisitions. Let's talk about the Papacy and Spain. I will try to make the ages and the dates less confusing, if I can. Very little was written about the Spanish Inquisition in the Dark Ages and the early Middle Ages which overlap. The Inquisitions continued into the 20th century AD."

"The 20th century," exclaimed Grace.

"Yes, we will delve into that in a little bit," said Zeus. "In the early Middle Ages, the 5th through the 10th centuries, between the fall of Rome and the Renaissance, and the Dark Ages, there was a time of good versus evil because of the era's lack of Christianity. And then in the Middle Ages there was the corruption within the Roman Catholic Church. A period when Popes ruled as kings, which created institutionalized lack of morality and hypocrisy. The Dark Ages ended around 1046 under the Gregorian Reform of Pope Clement II."

"The Age of Enlightenment of the 17th and 18th centuries AD saw religion become unreasonable. Enlightenment did not apply to the church as Inquisitions were still being conducted. The first of the Inquisitions began around 1184 AD and they were known as the Papal Inquisitions. The Spanish Inquisitions did not begin until around 1230 AD."

"Pope Alexander IV, around 1258 AD, is said to have limited Inquisitions to those presumed to be of heretical belief. That, of course, was decided by the church. The Roman Catholic saw witches and those who committed harm by magic as evil as or equal to Satan. Witches were blamed for the Hundred Years War and the Black Death. Also, for four centuries, witches were blamed for climate conditions. That was from the 15th to the 19th centuries AD."

"Witches were not the only prey of the Catholics. Under the Papal Inquisition of 1391 AD, hundreds of Jews were killed, and their synagogue was destroyed in the town of Seville. The Papal Inquisitions continued until King Ferdinand II of Aragon and Queen Isabella I of Castile established their Spanish Inquisition. The Spanish Inquisition included the territories of the Canary Islands, the Spanish Netherlands, the Kingdom of Naples, and as I mentioned before, the Americas. But, squeezed in there, was the Episcopal Inquisition around 1184 to 1230 AD. I told you the dates were confusing. However, the dates are not important as it is to know all of this was perpetrated in the name of the Christian

God. They were ruthless with their discrimination, not to mention the killings."

"I do not remember there being so many Inquisitions. I thought it was only Spain, and Catholic … but the Episcopalians," said Grace.

"The Spanish Inquisition was probably the biggest and worst of all the Inquisitions. The Spanish Inquisition held court in Hispanic America from 1830 AD until the end of the Inquisition period for Spain in 1834 AD. The last execution took place in 1826 AD. However, the Papacy held Inquisitions until 1908 AD."

"In 1908. People were killed until 1908?" asked Grace.

"Imprisoned," replied Zeus.

"How many people were killed?" asked Grace.

"That is a hard one to pin down," replied Zeus. "Historically, there is no one solid reference as to the number of victims executed throughout the Spanish Empire, but it is sizeable. Worse, there were those who deny the Inquisitions even took place at all. Here is what Cardinal George Cottier, of the Vatican had to say about the Inquisitions, 'You can't ask pardon for deeds which aren't there'. Even with the proof, I guess his remarks confirm that faith causes denial."

"Then, on the other side of the coin. In 'Ten things you should know about the Inquisition' it reads, 'Torture was an integral part of the Inquisitional process, mainly to extract confessions – just as it was part of the system used by the secular courts of the time'."

"It is hard to conceive that the church condoned torture by saying if it is alright for the police, it is permissible by the church," said Grace.

"Essentially, you are right," said Zeus. "But torture was not used until twenty years into the Inquisition, when circa 1252 AD Pope Innocent IV allowed it."

"How does anyone know that?" asked Grace.

"No one really does," replied Zeus. "And claims, only 100, were burned at the stake, out of 125,000 trials ... a nice even number. The Vatican justified torture by stating that they did not torture for more than 15 minutes."

"Oh, I see, they all had wristwatches. So, that made it alright," said Grace.

"Here are some more statistics. Two guys named Henningsen and Contreras seemed to have conducted a study and found that out of 44,674 Inquisitions only 826 people ended up having been executed."

"It may not seem important to the Most Holy Roman Catholic Church, but it certainly was to those 826. I use Most Holy, loosely," said Grace.

"Then," began Zeus. "This guy, Monter, came up with but 1,000 executions between 1300 until 1630 AD. Again, a nice round number. Then, a fellow named Kaman claims that only, yes only, 2,000 executions took place in all of the Spanish Inquisitions."

"Another author, Beaumont, posits that the 350 years of the Spanish Inquisition; it really lasted longer than that ... anyway ... he states that 'only' 3,000 to 5,000 were executed. He is supposedly debunking legends."

"Notice, these historians attempt to sweep the horror of this under the rug A little more creditable was a Spanish secretary to the Inquisition named Llorente, 1756 to 1823 AD. He stated that the number of heretics burned at the stake was 32,000. Another author states that the executions number 3,000 to 10,000 with as many as 125,000 dying due to torture and horrid treatment in prisons."

"Llorente's number of 32,000 burned at the stake and 125,000 dying in the prisons seems more believable or as good as the stats can get," said Grace.

"I agree," said Zeus. "Just think, as late as 1908 AD, the Papal Inquisitions ended with the Vatican's Congregation of the Inquisition. This august group was renamed the Congregation for the Doctrine of the Faith. But, it wasn't until 2000 that the Pope apologized for the unnecessary violence used. He went on to say, 'the image of the Inquisition represents almost a symbol of a scandal'."

"Almost a symbol of a scandal? How deplorable ... lame," said Grace.

"Then, there was the New England Inquisition," said Zeus.

"The Salem witch trials? Right?" said Grace.

"In what would become the colonies, from February 1692 until May 1693 AD, things weren't much better as fourteen women and six men were executed as heretics. And, the Catholics didn't fair well either. Christopher Hitchens, in his book 'god is not Great', wrote, 'Theocracy had just entered the English language – and to the Puritans, it was a good concept. They forbade Church of England clergy from setting foot in their new American theocracy in Boston and Salem, hung Quakers, and passed a law to hang any Catholic priests who might show up'."

"Congress shall make no law ..."

"The Constitution ... the First Amendment?" said Grace.

"Yes," continued Zeus. "Congress shall make no law respecting the establishment of religion or prohibiting the free exercise thereof; or abridging the freedom of speech, or of the press; or the right of the people peaceably to assemble, and to petition the government for a redress of grievances. Few realize that there is no reference to God in our Constitution. But, it took until 1963, to ban Bible readings in public schools. However, President Eisenhower asked congress to put 'under God' in the pledge of allegiance as an anti-communist gesture. 'Under God' is still in the pledge. A joint resolution of Congress was also signed by President Eisenhower. While still in office, effective 30 July 1956, the words 'In God We Trust' were placed on paper currency. It is still on the bills today. However, the Freedom from Religion Foundation is suing to have 'under God' removed from the pledge, and 'In God We Trust' removed from all money; bills and coins.

"All of this information about the Inquisitions begs for questions to be answered ... and with serious thought. Why was the Papacy and the fiefdoms so eager to tie young women to a stake, pile wood around them and burn them to death? Why is the Ku Klux Klan a Christian organization? Why are entire cultures of our citizenry, the recipients of so much hate? Why did a mass of white-supremacists march around a synagogue in Charlottesville, Virginia, with torches chanting, 'Jews will not replace us'? Why do a bunch of men parade around shirtless to show off their swastika tattoos? Why do peace loving Buddhists, kill Muslims in Myanmar?"

"'Why', you ask.? I think the answer is simple, but also perplexing. It has to do with all the different religions," said Grace

"Yes, it is that simple. The believer in the different religions have faith that it is the gods telling them to do it. They are being told by god to slash and burn their way to heaven. If our nation did not have the laws it has today, do you doubt New Englanders would not hang witches and warlocks? The Papal Inquisition ended in 1908 AD, but what if the Italian laws had not stopped the insanity? Do you think the Vatican would still be burning them at the stake? A scary thought. With the Vatican considering itself a separate country, the Papacy and staff do and say what pleases them. For example, the Pope has not admitted to the last Inquisitions except as a 'symbol of scandal'. The Pope is the vicar of the Messiah; the Roman Catholic Messiah not the Jewish Messiah. After all, to Catholics, only Catholics can go to heaven."

"Sadly, these gods do not create loving, understanding, caring, forgiving, charitable people. These gods and their revealed-religion are created by homo sapiens. It is because of the homo sapiens who walk the Earth that these conjured gods exist. It is all made-up. From the beginning of religions, what has been created? In the name of God, it is a path to a rabble of psychopaths, constantly on the war-path, to kill, to plunder, not to mention the taking of virgins as spoils of war. Don't forget the pedophile priests abusing pre-pubescent children. We haven't discussed this despicable time in the history of the Roman Catholic church. The cardinals, arch-bishops, and bishops knew about these child abusers and did nothing but move them from parish to parish. The world should be angry about these behaviors, not putting money into collection plates. And, it goes on today with little or no remorse from the leaders of the Catholic Church. Disgraceful!"

"Zeus, this is the first time I have seen you so animated," said Grace.

"Yes, I suppose so," began Zeus. "When a death-row inmate is walking those last steps to the execution chamber, a chaplain is walking with the inmate, praying for the inmate's soul. To me, and many others, added to the distain, is that an execution by the state appears on the death certificate as 'homicide'. Even more disgraceful, is that the government condones, as did the Vatican, the taking of a human life as punishment. We should label this period of supposed justifiable killing; the Modern Inquisition."

"I think executions reprehensible," said Grace.

"They smack of the Dark Ages," said Zeus.

"I think we have had enough for tonight, don't you, Zeus?" asked Grace.

"I agree. We will continue tomorrow night," replied Zeus.

"What's on the agenda?" asked Grace.

"Contradictions - man's inhumanity to man, in the name of gods.," replied Zeus. "Night, Grace"

"Night, Zeus."

CHAPTER EIGHTEEN

IT DOESN'T SAY THAT IN THE OTHER VERSE

"Good evening."

"We are starting early tonight, aren't we?" asked Grace.

"Yes, we are. We have a lot to cover. We may not get our talk completed in one night," replied Zeus.

"I am ready," said Grace.

"Okay, here goes," began Zeus. "When a contradiction is found in the scriptures, it is common to take the kindest verse read as the truth, and, perhaps disregard other verses. An example, creationism is taught in parochial school as science. And, then the student starts studying in college and is met head on with evolution. The student may not be inclined to accept evolution as science. Or, the student would disregard it all together, as evolution is not the 'written word of God'. A student from Pakistan probably will not believe in the same God as the student from Boston. One being Muslim and the other, being perhaps, Roman Catholic. It may be the same way for the Bible. One might believe the first creation story, but not the second. After all, if the person is not Jewish and has never heard of The Talmud, that person would not know of Lilith."

"While researching the topic of contradictions, I found 832 in the Christian Bible. The contradictions give weight to the argument that The Tanach,

The New Testament, and The Book of Mormon are not perfect. Of course, we have proven that to be true, already, right?"

"Yes, I suppose so," said Grace.

"Don't worry, you will lose that spark ... that ember ... before we finish," said Zeus.

"The spark is already closer to an ember than a spark," said Grace.

"Good," said Zeus. "Jeremiah 8:8, *'How can you say we are wise and Hashem's Torah is with us? The quill writes its falsehood as the scribes are false'*. Then onto, *'Proverbs 30:5-6, 'Every word of God is refined; He is a shield to those who trust Him. Add not to His words, for He will find that you have deceived'*.*"

"The Jeremiah verse calls the scribes false and the Proverbs verses gives a warning, but both refer to fictitious writings."

"The prophecies of the Messiah, according to the Christian faith, do not jibe with the prophecies of The Tanach."

"The Christian Old Testament, and most Christians do not know this this verse or that it is from the Tanach. First, Isaiah 7:14, *'Therefore my Lord Himself will give you a sign: Behold the she will be with child and bear a son, and she will name him Immanuel'*.*"

"Now, from The Tanach. And Isaiah 9:5, *'For a child has been born to us, a son has been given to us, and the dominion will rest on his shoulder; the Wonderous Adviser, Mighty God, Eternal Father, called his name Sar-Shalom'*. Sar-Shalom means prince of peace."

"You'll find a similar prophesy in The Old Testament in Micah 5:2, *'Therefore He will deliver them'*, meaning deliver them to their enemies, *'until the time that a woman in childbirth gives birth; then the rest of his brothers will return with the children of Israel'.*"

"And, again, from The Tanach. Zechariah 9:9, *'Rejoice greatly, O daughter of Zion! Shout for joy, O daughter of Jerusalem! Behold your king will come to you, righteous and victorious is he, a humble man riding on a donkey'.*"

"Now let's go to the coming of the Messiah ... hear all the verses in The New Testament that talks of his coming. Matthew 1:23, *'Behold, the virgin will be with child and will bear a Son, and they will call him Immanuel'.*"

"Matthew 1:25, where it reads Joseph took Mary as his wife, *'... but kept her a virgin until she gave birth to a Son; and he called his name Jesus'.*"

"Matthew 2:1, *'Now after Jesus was born in Bethlehem in the days* of King *Herod'*, remember King Herod in the days of Jesus."

"Luke 1:31, *'Behold, you will be pregnant in your womb. You will bear a son and his name will be Jesus'.*"

"It appears that the prophecies came to fruition as The Tanach story and The New Testament stories are similar as they neatly match, except that is, for the names. The child, in The New Testament, was named Jesus, not Immanuel. Jesus means 'God saves'. Jesus in Hebrew is Yeshua and in Greek Jesus is Iesous. Immanuel also spelled Emmanuel, is not a title but a name; it means God is with us. So, in The New Testament the proper name for Jesus should have been Jesus Immanuel, meaning 'God saves' and 'God is with us'. Was this a mistake? Was it prophecy? Or, merely copied?" asked Zeus. "No one knows."

"With what you are saying it appears the names were not copied correctly … I don't know. What was the Herod thing?" asked Grace.

"Remember?" asked Zeus.

"I think so, but could you please review it," said Grace

"Although some would consider these as contradictions. I see them simply as different explanations of the same story. And, this has to do with timing … getting the dates correct. Jesus was born in the year 1 BC. But, Herod died in 4 BC. Well into 600 AD, the calendar was changed to reflect that Jesus was born in 6 BC which according to Christians would have Jesus born six years before 1 Anno Domini; six years before his era. The calendars were changed to fit the King Herod mistake sometime around the 7th century. Also, there is a contradiction as to where Jesus was taken after the Herod proclamation."

"In the New Testament, Matthew 2:13, *'An angel appeared to Joseph and said, 'Get thee out of Bethlehem with Jesus and Mary and flee to Egypt and stay there until I tell you. Herod is going to search his kingdom and kill the child'.*"

"But, in Luke 2:39-40, *'When all was according to the laws of God. Joseph, Mary, and Jesus returned to Galilee, to their home in Nazareth. And there they lived as the child grow with God's grace upon him'.* One verse has Jesus being taken to Egypt and another to Nazareth."

"Ah, that's really a big difference. All these years, I never questioned why those passages were different, until now. The writers didn't have their stories straight," said Grace. "And, all of this is fine. However, I never noticed the differences, of supposedly, the same stories. I just overlooked the contradictions. I never questioned any of the differences."

"Most never realize the difference in the passages," replied Zeus. "Here is another. It has to do with the method of transportation for Jesus to get to Jerusalem. Matthew 21:6-7, '*The disciples did just as Jesus told them to do. They brought a donkey and a colt; they then laid their coats on them; and He sat on the coats*'. It does not say which animal Jesus rode. Now, to Luke 19:33-35, '*As they were untying the colt, its owners said to them, 'Why are you untying the colt?' They said, 'The Lord has need of it'. They brought it to Jesus, and they threw their coats on the colt and put Jesus on it*'."

"It was a colt, they just took the colt?" asked Grace. "And to think all of these years, I thought he rode on the back of a donkey. That's interesting … no one pointed out that the colt was stolen. A colt was stolen for Jesus to ride and all of that artwork that shows him on a donkey … and it is laughable, you can't even ride on the back of a colt. What is the truth?"

Yet how many realize the contradiction? Does it really matter? Probably not, it is all a myth anyway," replied Zeus."

"Follow these two verses," said Zeus. "This is a major difference, a major contradiction. Even though the time of day is different with one saying the ninth hour and the other the sixth hour, the real difference has to do

with what Jesus cried out on the cross. To the fundamentalists, his last words are different, and unexplained. One outcry is of anger, the other acceptance "In Matthew 27:45-46, *'Now from the sixth hour of darkness fell upon the land until the ninth hour. About the ninth hour Jesus cried out, 'Eli, Eli, Lama sabachthai?'.'*"

"Yes" said Grace.

"It means, 'My God, my God, why have you forsaken me?', said Zeus. "Now, to the contradiction. In Luke 23:44-46, *'It was now about the six hour and darkness fell over the whole land until the ninth hour, because the sun was obscured; and the veil of the temple was torn in two. And Jesus cried out in a loud voice, 'Father into your hands I commit my Spirit'. Having said this Jesus took his last breath'.*"

"I never paid any attention to the differences. I was never taught the Matthew verses, only the 'forsaken me' quote," said Grace.

"Have you been keeping track of how many times you have said you were never taught that?" asked Zeus.

"Not consciously. But, now, that you mention it, that probably explains why the ember is getting cooler," replied Grace.

"There are contradictions in the commandments. Two are in Exodus only a few verses apart. They are not only contradictory, Exodus 25:18, violates the second commandment," said Zeus. "In Exodus 20:4, *'You will not make a graven image or any likeness of that which is in heaven or of the Earth below or in the deepness of the waters'.*"

"Exodus 25:18 reads, *'You will hammer out two Cherubim of gold and place them at both ends of the cover'*. The cover is the canopy over the tabernacle."

"I know about that one and remember questioning why the difference in the same book," said Grace.

"Cherubims, as written in the scriptures are in the heavens and are guardians of paradise," said Zeus. "Here is another contradiction that has to do with war and peace. In Exodus 15:3, *'Hashem is the master of war'*, and in Romans 15:33, *'It is the will of the God of peace to be with you'*."

"Interesting … war and peace," said Grace.

"Now, delve into the most noteworthy of all biblical contradictions," said Zeus. "Here is the contradiction in the form of a question. Can you get there by 'works' alone? Or, does it take 'faith' alone?"

"I have no idea," replied Grace.

"Romans 3:19-20,28, *'Whatever the law reads, it is written for those who are under the law. Be accountable to God by saying nothing; because by the works of the law no flesh will be justified in his sight; it is by the law that the knowledge of sin comes to man. Man is justified by faith apart from the works of the law'*," said Zeus.

"And in Romans 5:1, *'Having been justified by faith there is a calm brought to man by his Lord Jesus Christ'*."

"But, in James 2:24, it reads. *'Man is justified by his works, not by faith alone. Was not the harlot Rehab justified by works after receiving the messengers and sent them out another way? A body without spirit is dead; faith without works is also dead'."*

"These verses have caused Christian clergy a continuous challenge of trying to justify, reconcile, rationalize, and account for their way around this one. A quote from Penn Jillette provides the best explanation for unraveling this or any contradiction. Penn said, 'When someone tries to interpret something for you, they always have an agenda'. And one last word from The Tanach," said Zeus. "And, it has to do with timing from the Vaticanus Septuagint. Methuselah dies at the age of 969 in 2256 BC. This just happens to be 14 years after the flood; and he was not on the ark. This is a bigger math error than Herod's death year."

"These contradictions and time discrepancies, if really addressed in earnest, could play havoc with biblical writings. I wonder if they can ever be reconciled and if so, by whom?" asked Grace

"Grace this is a small sampling of the hundreds of contradictions in The Tanach and The New Testament. And with time, more will probably be uncovered. Now, onto The Books of Mormonism. Even though about 70% of The Book of Mormon is derived from the Christian Bible, it contradicts much that is in The New Testament and The Tanach. Joseph Smith tried, but did a poor job, of using the King's English. One cannot help but laugh when told the Book of Mormon contains over two thousand repetitions of the phrase, 'and it came to pass'. And, as we talked about, there are scores of contradictions in The Book of Mormon. But, the real interest is in the contradictions between and among the three books of Mormonism; The Book of Mormon, Doctrine and Covenants, and Pearl of Great Price.

Smith wrote the latter books to expand upon his original book, and, thus, created confusion among the books as the writings did not agree."

Zeus continued, "Many try to compare the Bible with Smith's books. It is an effort in futility. The Books of Mormon served but one man; Joseph Smith Junior."

"Oy vay," laughed Grace. "Oh, go ahead."

"Pearl of Great Price, Moses 3:8, *'And I, the Lord God, planted a garden eastward in Eden, and there I put the man whom I had formed'.*"

"Now, to *Doctrine and Covenants,* section 107:53, *'Spring Hill,* that's in Indiana, *'is named by the Lord Adam-ondi-Ahman, because said He, it is a place where Adam shall come to visit his people, or the Ancient of Days shall sit, as spoken of by Daniel the prophet'.* Later Smith moves the Mormon garden of Eden to Far West, Missouri; having had to run from the law."

"Good grief," said Grace.

"I agree," replied Zeus.

"Now, to The Book of Mormon, Alma 11:27-29, *'And Ameluk said: Yea, here is a true and living God. Now Zeezrom said: Is there more than one God? And he answered, No'.*"

"Doctrine and Covenants, Section 121:32, *'According to that which was ordained in the midst of the Council of the Eternal God of all other Gods before this world was, that should be reserved unto the finishing and the end thereof, when every man shall enter into his eternal presence and into his immortal rest'."*

"I take it you are going somewhere with this," said Grace.

"For sure, for sure," said Zeus. "Doctrine and Covenants, Section 132:20, *'Then shall they be Gods, because they have no end; therefor they shall be from everlasting to everlasting, because they continue; then shall they be above all, because all things are subject unto them. Then shall they be Gods, because they have all power, and the angels are subject to them'."*

"So, who becomes gods?" asked Grace.

"All those that have reached celestial heaven. Hang on," replied Zeus. "Pearl of Great Price, Abraham 4:1, *'And the Lord said; Let us go down. And they went down at the beginning, and they, that is the Gods, organized and formed the heavens and the Earth'."*

"Did you put the phrase, 'that is the gods' in there?" asked Grace.

"Nope, Smith put it in there," replied Zeus. "Let's talk about these gods a bit more. The Book of Mormon, Alma 18:26-28, *'And then Ammon said: Believest thou that there is a Great Spirit? And he said, Yea. And Ammon said: This is God. And Ammon said unto him again Believest thou this Great Spirit, who is God, created all things which are in heaven and in the Earth'."*

"Catch this. The contradiction is in Alma, God created the heavens and the Earth. But, here, we read that it took three. Notice the word 'they' in Pearl of Great Price, Abraham 4:1, *'And the Lord said: Let us go down. And* 'they' went down at the beginning, and' they', that is the Gods, organized and formed the heavens and the Earth'."

"They?" asked Grace.

"The three gods. That is why I accentuated the 'they'," said Zeus. "The father, son, and holy ghost."

"Doctrine and Covenants, Section 130:22, 'The father has a body of flesh and bones as tangible as man's; the Son also, but the Holy Ghost has not a body of flesh and bone, but is a personage of Spirit. Were it not so, the Holy Ghost could not dwell in us'."

"In Mormonism, there are three separate Gods; the father and the son are as real as humans and the holy spirit is the soul. Now, onto the changing word," said Zeus. The Book of Mormon, Alma 41:8, 'Now, the decrees of God are unalterable; therefore, the way is prepared that whosoever will, may walk therein and be saved'."

"This one will throw you off ... it is so totally out of character from the rest of the books. Doctrine and Covenants, Section 56:4-5, 'Wherefore I, the Lord, command and revoke, as it seemeth me good; and all this to be answered upon the heads of the rebellious, saith the Lord. Wherefore, I revoke the commandment which was given unto thy servants Thomas B. Marsh, that he shall take up his journey speedily to the land of Missouri, and my servant Selah J. Griffin shall also go with him'. In these verses a commandment is revoked and God names specific individuals to go to, of all places, Missouri, which is the place of Smith's New Zion."

"Smith was almost hanged in Missouri and was run out of the state, yet he keeps going back to that place. If not him, he sends others there. It makes no sense," said Grace.

"A lot in the Mormon books does not make sense. Now more about polygamy. The Book of Mormon, Jacob 2:24, *'Behold, David and Solomon truly had many wives and concubines, which thing was abominable before me, saith the Lord'.*"

"Doctrine and Covenants, Section 132:38, *'David also received many wives and concubines, and also Solomon and Moses many servants, as also many others of my servants, from the beginning of creation until this time; and in nothing did they sin save in those things which they received not from me'.*"

"It seems to me Smith did not remember his earlier works," said Grace.

"Doctrine and Covenants, Section 132:61, *'And again, as pertaining to the law of the priesthood – if any man espouse a virgin, and desire to espouse another, and the first give her consent, and if he espouses the second, and they are virgins, and have vowed to no other man, then is he justified; he cannot commit adultery for they are given unto him; for he cannot commit adultery with that that belongeth unto him and to no one else'.*"

"Smith obviously did not care for what he dictated in The Book of Mormon about polygamy, so he changed it in Doctrines and Covenants. There is nothing in the books of Mormon that allow the taking of another man's wife. Smith must have just made that up to suit himself."

"Ah, but the real pathway to heaven for the LDS Church goers is in The Book of Mormon, Mormon 8:32, *'Yea, it shall come in a day when there shall be churches built up that shall say: Come unto me, and for your money you shall be forgiven all your sins'.* The church is forgiving sins for indulgences, ala the Roman Catholic Church. Then, in Doctrine and Covenants, Section 64:23, *'Behold, now it is called today until the coming of the Son of Man, and verily it is a day of sacrifice, and a day for tithing of my people: for he that is tithed shall not be burned at his coming'."*

"There is no contradiction in the two references as to tithing. Those references are of the two most important tenets of Mormonism. That is, tithing will get you to heaven. And the second is, those that attain the level of celestial heaven will be made gods. Another important tenet is that the father, the son, and the holy spirit are three separate gods making Mormonism polytheistic. And it is polytheism we will delve into tomorrow night," said Zeus.

"And what would that be?" asked Grace.

"Hinduism," replied Zeus. "And, you will be surprised as to the myriad of gods. Gods upon gods upon gods," said Zeus.

"And I will keep that in my head, word-for-word?" asked Grace.

"So far, that is a true statement," replied Zeus. "Next, I want us to talk about Hinduism and Buddhism. So, we will discuss the Hindus tomorrow. Don't forget group. Night, for now," said Zeus.

"Bye, bye."

CHAPTER NINETEEN

SO MANY GODS

"How are you tonight?" asked Zeus.

"I am fine, thank-you," replied Grace.

"Oh, I see … frantic, insecure, neurotic, and emotional," said Zeus.

"Yes, that about sums it up," laughed Grace.

"You will be out of this place before you know it," said Zeus.

"I'm gonna get sprung?" asked Grace.

"In less than ten days," replied Zeus.

"That is good news to start the evening," said Grace.

"Yes, but don't think about that. Let's concentrate on Hinduism," said Zeus.

"Okay, continue," said Grace.

"'In Hinduism, unlike the conceptualization of God in monotheistic religions such as Christianity, Brahman God, does not interact with human lives'."

"Sounds like Deism," said Grace.

"'Gods descend to this world in some form whenever there is unacceptable imbalance between good and evil'. Both quotes are from

Doctor Amrutur V. Srinvasan," said Zeus. "Hinduism has one God, a supreme pantheistic being. Yet, Hinduism is a polytheistic religion."

"It makes no sense," said Grace.

"You are right ... it doesn't ... but ... well ... just follow along," replied Zeus. "Hindus are a people, originally from the banks of the Indus river. The name Hindu is derived from Persian. Supposedly, Hinduism began around six thousand BC, which makes Hinduism the oldest religion in the world."

"To be concise, Hinduism is not understandable. The religion, with a billion strong, has so many aspects, so many gods, one cannot keep up. All a Hindu has to do is take some clay, make a statue of a new god, and pray to it."

"Although Srinvasan writes that Brahman is a pantheistic god; Brahman is not, as there are other principle gods," began Zeus.

"Brahman is a god that defies description. Brahman is the universe, a timeless being, formless, divine, and the creator."

"Vishnu is the sustainer of the created universe."

"Shiva is the god of the next time cycle of the universe. Also, the destroyer. And, a consort to Devi."

"Saraswati is the goddess of learning."

Laksmi is the consort of Vishnu and is the goddess of wealth."

"Devi is creative power and the consort of Shiva."

'Ganapati, also called Ganesha, is the elephant headed god and is the presiding god over the New York City Hindu Temple Society."

"Jyotisha is known as the astronomer and as the astrologer. Deities are invoked during rituals and studied by astrologers who provide horoscopes at a child's birth. Hindu festivals are tied to the lunar calendar. The most straightforward system of house division comes from Hindu astrology. Once Hindus determine their rising sun, they then divide their houses by 12 in keeping with the horoscope wheel," said Zeus.

"Surya is the sun god."

"Chandra is the moon god."

"Budha, with one 'd' not two as in Buddha, is the god of Mercury."

"Vayu is the wind god."

"Varuna is the water god."

"Okay, enough with the gods already," laughed Grace.

"What's so funny?" asked Zeus.

"This is supposed to be a monotheistic religion," replied Grace.

"The gods go on and on. There are thousands of them in the Hindu scriptures. There are Hindu gods as individuals, families, villagers, and temple goers. They all just make up gods to pray to for their needs."

"Sounds as if it is paganism," said Grace.

"You are right. Hinduism goes from pantheism, to polytheism, to paganism," replied Zeus. "You thought the god's list was getting to you ... well ... let me list some definitions."

"I am listening. I am a little disappointed in myself," said Grace.

"Why?" asked Zeus.

"I am becoming very judgmental," replied Grace.

"No, you are thinking rationally. Really, you are starting to reason things through. You are working through the last of the ember," said Zeus. "Now, to the definitions. Some of these will be familiar sounding."

"Bhagavad Gita is called 'The Songs of the Lord'; it is the Hindu manual for spiritual life."

"Their scripture?" asked Grace.

"Yes, it is the scripture I alluded to," replied Zeus.

"On to Puranas which are stories of the Gods."

"Dharma is to hold or to sustain."

"Veda are sacred books. Veda means to know."

"Upanishads are a part of the Vedas meaning something below the surface. They are the intellectual philosophy of the Vedas."

"Truth is the ultimate goal of Hinduism and truth can be experienced in countless ways."

"Karma ..."

"Ah, the big one," said Grace.

"We will see karma, again. Essentially, in simple terms, karma means a spiritual 'what goes around, comes around', from reincarnation to reincarnation. Karma can be many lifetimes apart. Karma can be positive as well as negative. From Srinvasan again, 'Acrions of the soul, while residing in a body, require that it reap the consequences of those actions in the next life – the same soul in a different body'."

"Moksha is the release of the truthful, purified soul that merges with the Brahman and becomes pure spirit; no longer reincarnated."

"Hare Krishnas were saffron robed, shaved head, collectors of money at airports in the seventies. Krishna is the avatar, the manifestation of deity, of Vishnu.

Bhu is Earth.

Bhuwa, suva, maha, jana, tapa, and satya are levels of heaven."

"Six. Twice as many as the Mormons," said Grace.

"Yes, but this really gets confusing. Follow along. Atala, bitala, sutala, talatala, rasatala, mahatala, and patala are the seven levels of heaven."

"Thirteen levels of heaven?" asked Grace.

"I guess so. I can't find the reason for the two sets of levels," said Zeus. "I described the Vedas as the closest writings that can be loosely considered scriptures. But, let's refer to them as scriptures. The Vedas are the orthodox scriptures of Hinduism. The Vedas are broken down into many parts. The first is mantras. Then comes benedictions, rituals, ceremonies, and sacrifices. Followed by meditation, spirituality, and philosophy. And then the last is the Upanishads. The Vedas were written in various time periods ranging from 1,700 BC until the first century of the common era. Before Sanskrit, the Vedas were passed along orally, which leaves a lot of interpretation through the ages. Manuscripts did not stop at the first century. Manuscripts were still being written and discovered as late as the 14th century AD. As with Jewish and Christian texts, the Vedas were passed orally and then written down as the centuries went by. There is no one source of writing that make up the Vedas."

"The Upanishads," began Zeus, "were composed around 800 BC through the 15th century AD. They, too, were written from oral tradition. The Upanishads define that the self is the only reality, yet they portend that the self is dual and non-dual as with silence and sound, white and black, I and thou; one cannot be realized without the other. Yet, reality is not classifed. It is the 'reality' of the Upanishads that could have been taken from the writings of Buddhism, especially the later manuscripts. In the Upanishads, as with the writings of Buddhism, which we will discuss later, 'reality' is a very elusive entity."

"As with all scriptures, the Vedas and the Upanishads are just books, no different from Exodus, Matthew and the Mormon Book of Alma. All written by men, edited, and with many versions."

"The central point of Hinduism is the universe and 'atman' which is the grounding of being. In the search for reality, it requires one to give up one's name and take a spiritual name. To grasp reality, one must become a nobody; no one and all one, and abandon society and live only a spiritual life. Yet, reality cannot be and is not defined in the Vedas or the

Upanishads. Reality is to be defined by Hindus themselves. This begs the question as to 'reality' and 'truth'; when does one know when evasive reality and mystical truth are found?"

"Reality and truth. Who in Hinduism defines it?" asked Grace.

"No one and it cannot be defined by one's self. Essentially, according to Hinduism, reality and truth are not to be found, yet the Vedas and the Upanishads cannot define either and the Hindus are left on their own," replied Zeus.

"To define what cannot be explained?" asked Grace.

"And around and around we go," replied Zeus. "How about some potpourri?"

"You know I love potpourri," replied Grace.

Ganapati or Ganesha, you can use either name. Anyway, Ganesha was told to guard his mother's house and let no one in. Shiva became enraged and cut off Ganesha's head with a sword. Shiva then wanted a head that was pointed south to replace Ganesha's head. All that could be found was a sleeping elephant with its head pointed south. Well, the elephant's head was cut off and placed on Ganesha's neck. That is how Ganesha ended up with an elephant's head."

"I wondered were that creature came from," said Grace.

"Shiva was disturbed by Kama Deva, who is Cupid, so Shiva opened a third eye and burned Kama to ashes."

"The red dot on a Hindu woman's forehead represents a family in harmony, but also a third eye. The third eye represents Shiva."

"Brahma has four legs and four arms and is different from Brahman. Brahma is the egg that hatched the universe and is the progenitor of all beings."

"The swastika is an ancient Hindu sign meaning the continuum of life."

"In Indian, pajama means a long coat. The British changed the word to mean nightwear."

"All the Gods worshiped by Hindus represent the Brahman."

"Hinduism has no founder."

"Hindus worship cows, monkeys, snakes, trees, and plants."

"Hindus believe in the intimate connection between Atman, which are individual souls, and Rahman."

"There are no male or female spirits."

"Hindu religious leaders include sages, austere and spiritual like believers; and swamis, religious leaders belonging to one of hundreds of Hindu orders."

"Indians speak nearly 20 languages and hundreds of dialects."

"Maharishi Mahesh Yogi taught that bliss is our birthright."

"Hinduism has four personal divisions. The first is dharma, to sustain; then morsha, salvation; kama, fulfillment; and artha, wealth and fame."

"You must be born into Hinduism. You cannot convert."

"The post-Vedic era is 500 BC to 500 AD when Hindu broke into four denominations. Thus, Vedic Sanskrit scriptures are not in line with the philosophy of all four."

"Even though the caste system has been outlawed, it is still practiced to include 'honor killings' of daughters that marry into a lower caste."

"At one-time, widows were cremated along with their deceased husbands."

"Two tenets of Hinduism are; if you destroy you've nothing from which to create. And, believe in yourself. And if you believe in yourself you believe in god."

"The god that does not intervene in the universe?" asked Grace.

"The study of Hinduism is very confusing. Trying to patch an 'anything goes' philosophy with god upon god, each having a different meaning is a task. I will finish with this quote from the British scholar, Sir Monier Monier-Williams, 'It is a creed based on an original, simple, pantheistic doctrine, but branching out into an endless variety of polytheistic superstitions. Like the sacred fig-tree of India, which from a single stem sends out numerous branches destined to send roots to the ground and become trees themselves, until the parent stock is lost in a dense forest of its own offshoots, so has this pantheistic creed rooted itself firmly in the Hindu mind, and spread its ramifications so luxuriantly that the simplicity of its root dogma is lost in an exuberant outgrowth of monstrous mythology."

"Wow. Ol' Monier, Monier knew how to draw out a sentence. I am glad you have that quote. It puts into writing what I was thinking, but I could not get my confused head around it. Not the quote, but Hinduism altogether.," said Grace.

"Well, here we are," said Zeus.

"Well, here we are," laughed Grace. "Are we done with Hinduism?"

"Yes," replied Zeus.

"So, what is next?" asked Grace.

"The Buddha," replied Zeus.

"Beautiful. I have always been intrigued by Buddhism. I am looking forward to it," said Grace.

"Good. Talk to you tomorrow night."

"Until the morrow."

CHAPTER TWENTY

PERHAPS THE BUDDHA GOT IT RIGHT

"Are you ready," asked Zeus.

"Sure, but first, I have a question for you."

"Go ahead, ask away," replied Zeus
"We've spent all this time together and I don't know what you look like," said Grace.

"Does it matter?" asked Zeus.
"No, I guess not, not when you ask me if it matters. I guess that means the ember must still be with me a little. I wanted to 'see' what someone so wise and so all-knowing, like you, looked like," said Grace.

"That takes you back to your original questioning, doesn't it? The reason you ended up here," said Zeus.

"Yes, I suppose. I have always wondered what God looked like. Also, if God was a He or a She? But now, with the ember all but gone, I realize that all I knew, and I thought I understood was based on was good for me when it was less understood by me, when I didn't question it," said Grace.

"So, now that you have a better understanding, does it matter anymore what God looks like?" asked Zeus.

"No, because I now know that the understanding is beyond seeing God. There isn't the urgency or the ever demanding need to prove or disprove or see or not see. What is, is. So, I think I just answered my question about what you look like," said Grace.

"And, what is your answer?" asked Zeus.

"It doesn't matter what you look like. You are you. I am me. What is, is. I think, for the very first time, I realize I no longer need to rely on visual tokens, signs, or symbols to appreciate or understand our existence," replied Grace.

"Does this mean you don't believe in God anymore?" asked Zeus.

"It means I am free now to understand and appreciate the religions and all that have to offer mankind, but now, with an understanding and my eyes open. I don't feel judgmental about the different religions nor have I the feeling that I am being judged," said Grace.

"So, shall we continue?" asked Zeus.

"Yes, please," said Grace.

"Good. Now, we can study Buddhism. When a man in a wrap-around robe sits before you, cross-legged, with hands folded across his belly and tells you about his enlightenment, be assured the next thing to come is that you will not be enlightened in this lifetime, but, ah, he has been. He will begin to tell you oneness is Ananda; pure and unqualified knowledge is Prana. He will fill your head with words only he understands, or so he says," said Zeus.

"I am confused," said Grace.

"The Guru is confusing. That is the Guru's purpose. The Guru will ask you questions such as, 'What is the sound of one hand clapping?' or, "What did you look like before you were conceived?' Be aware Grasshopper, be aware Lotus Blossom, you are not being taught Buddhism, you are about to think in circles and become confused by trying to come to a meaning of it all which was not taught by The Buddha.

What this Guru, this 'teacher', is telling you comes from writings that were penned long after the death of The Buddha. Again, we have writings by unknown authors."

"Books by unknown authors seem to be a standard of revealed-religions," said Grace.

"However," began Zeus. "Buddhism is not a revealed-religion unless you believe the writings ranging from one hundred years after the death of The Buddha up until the 15th century AD. No one who knew The Buddha wrote a word about him and his teachings in his lifetime. The Buddha took The Middle Path. Who was he and how did he get there is not a mystery. There was no supernatural revelation; thus, Buddhism is not a revealed-religion. Or is it? More will be revealed. The teachings of The Buddha have to do with life's suffering. But, first, who was The Buddha?"

"A man asked the Dalai Lama about Buddhism and guilt. The Dalai Lama said, 'There is no guilt in Buddhism'. Suppose someone fails her elders and does not live up to her expectations, how would she feel? The Dalai Lama replied, 'It happens'."

"Siddhartha Gautama was born to a royal family in what is now Nepal. He was born into the Shakya clan. Prince Siddhartha was the pride of his father and was to be the next king. Siddhartha means, 'He whose aim is accomplished'. Now, here is where the writings of the texts, years after The Buddha died, try to make him a god, which he is not and never was."

"Supposedly, his mother, Queen Maya, went into solitude. A white six-tusked elephant came to her and touched her body. From that she became pregnant. She left the palace and went to her parent's home to have her child. Oh, but it was not a normal birth."

"Do tell,' laughed Grace.

"Prince Siddhartha was born, painlessly, from the side of his mother. As soon as Prince Siddhartha was born, he took seven steps to the north and proclaimed that this was his last lifetime."

"That sounds ridiculous," said Grace.

"I agree, but that is what the books say," says Zeus.

"It is almost silly. No, it is silly," said Grace.

"Anyway, Prince Siddhartha lived a charmed life in the palace but was not allowed to leave. Prince Siddhartha never ventured beyond the gates of the palace and he married at a very young age. He was soon to be the father of a son."

"Through song and poems, Prince Siddhartha heard of the wonders of the world but never experienced any of it, as he was palace-bound. But when Prince Siddhartha was twenty-nine, his father relented as he wanted the prince to see the kingdom over which he would someday reign. So, Prince Siddhartha ventured beyond the palace gates."

"The king arranged for it that the prince would see nothing negative in the village. But Prince Siddhartha and his charioteer came across a man bent over in pain. Prince Siddhartha asked what seemed to be the matter with the man. The charioteer told the prince that the man was ill. Prince Siddhartha had never experienced illness in anyone in the palace and was taken aback at the man's suffering. The next time the prince ventured into the village, he witnessed old age and death. He was devastated. On his last excursion, the prince knew what he had to do. He had to search for a way to end suffering and knew he would have to leave the palace and his family to do it. However, the king denied this and placed a guard on the prince to restrain him from leaving the palace. The guard fell asleep and the prince was able to slip out of the palace."

"Once away from the palace, Prince Siddhartha cut his hair and exchanged his clothes for a robe and started to roam the forest. Soon, he was in the company of two teachers who taught him meditation techniques. But soon, he found that meditation was not a deep enough understanding of how to relieve suffering. He knew he had to probe deeper into his mind."

Siddhartha went into the forest with five other celibates, those practicing self-denial. He fasted for six years. He ate little and was soon skin and bones. But, as he weakened, he realized he could not acquire the knowledge of which he was searching. He decided he had suffered for nothing. It was by a stream where he went to refresh himself that he discovered The Middle Path. He discovered his path was to live between self-indulgence and self-denial. His path was to live between the two extremes. This was the beginning of his understanding that all suffering of the mind comes from those two extremes."

"Siddhartha was offered some milk from a woman who had come into the forest. When the five celibates saw this, they became very disappointed in Siddhartha and left the forest. Siddhartha crossed the river and came upon a Bo tree, later known as the Bodhi tree, or the tree of enlightenment.

Siddhartha sat under the Bodhi tree. Mara, The Tempter, was horrified. She knew that if Siddhartha gained enlightenment, the delusion held over the minds of man would lose its power."

"Who the heck is Mara, The Tempter?" asked Grace.

"Mara, The Tempter, was a spirit that tried to tempt Siddhartha with one of her daughters. Mara was afraid that if Siddhartha became enlightened, the delusion held over the minds of man ... well ... would be gone."

"Siddhartha saw that envy, craving, greed, and all ignorance was the suffering of man. With that, Siddhartha became enlightened. He had become The Buddha. He had become 'the awakened one'."

"The Sanskrit word for suffering is 'duhkha'. It can also be translated as dissatisfaction. Thus, dissatisfaction comes about by things not being the way you wish them to be. Rather than use suffering, or duhkha, as for the Western mind, I will refer to it as dissatisfaction. This dissatisfaction brings us to The Four Noble Truths, which are the first of the teachings of the Buddha."

"It seems to me that The Middle Path is sane. I find the description of the Guru you talked about is a little ... well ... a little odd ... to say the least," said Grace.

"Gurus are mostly a sham and they want to confuse those that come to them. It makes the Gurus feel superior," replied Zeus.

"So, please, onto The Four Noble Truths. Sorry to interrupt," said Grace.

"I want you to stop me when you don't completely understand something," said Zeus. "Okay, The Four Noble Truths."

"The first Noble truth is suffering or dissatisfaction. It applies to all mental and emotional difficulties that arise through our lifetime. Even unpleasant events are considered dissatisfying, even though we cannot avoid them in our present being. The Buddha outlined these events as birth, aging, sickness, death, meeting with what you don't like, being parted from what you like, and especially, not getting what you want. This list covers everything in the human experience. The reason these dissatisfying events were chosen is the human ability to reduce everything to self-deception. Self-deception comes about by a person not wanting to look at the true self in that moment and the dissatisfaction continues moment by moment, second by second. It is our flawed nature that has us going from one dissatisfying event to another. It never stops, unless we can have it do so within ourselves."

"The Truth of the Cause of Dissatisfaction is The Second Noble Truth. The Buddha asks, 'What is the cause of all this misery? Where does it come from?' The Buddha answers the questions himself. 'It all comes from craving, from attachment, insatiable desires, and by these feelings, never knowing peace.'"

"One may think that dissatisfaction comes from misfortune or bad circumstances, or just bad luck, or for no reason at all. Steve Martin, in a comedy routine, asks five questions. He then gives a reason as the answer to the questions. The questions are, 'Why am I so wretched? Why am I so depraved? Why is my valium bill higher than my food bill? Why does jury duty pay more than my own job? Why is the only joy I know in life a dishwashing liquid?' Martin then goes on to tell the audience that they will have nothing in their lives for no reason at all. It's funny, but then again, it isn't. If you ask yourself questions such as those posed by Martin, you may indeed have put yourself in a wretched place."

"Example ... suppose you decide to up your social status and buy a luxury car to impress people? You really can't afford it, but you go into debt to purchase it. Now, you have a car that people will recognize and perhaps they will think of you as being rich. But, lo, you pull into the supermarket parking lot and aside of you is parked the same type of car. You are let down by knowing you are not that special at all. And, on top of it all, you will, for perhaps seventy-two months, have the dissatisfaction of a monthly car payment you really can't afford, and your insurance goes through the roof. A supernatural force did not bring the dissatisfaction upon you. You are experiencing The Truth of the Cause of Dissatisfaction. In the West, in the capitalist countries, materialism causes a great amount of dissatisfaction. Materialism and a perceived social status that is only given you by others that are dissatisfied with their climbing of the social ladder. But, there is a way to get away from all of this, all of the dissatisfaction, and suffer no more. That brings us to the next Noble Truth."

"The Third Noble Truth is The Truth of Dissatisfaction's Cessation. This Noble Truth will lead you to the 'cure' for your dissatisfaction; complete cessation. A millionaire was talking to another millionaire as they were watching a moving van being unloaded at a mansion in their cul-de-sac. The one millionaire said to the other, 'See that guy? The one by the van?

222

He is a billionaire'. The other millionaire replied, 'I pity him. He'll never have enough'."

"I get it. About two months ago a stock broker called me at home. She told me that an investment she offered was guaranteed to make me money. I think that is illegal. Anyway, I told her I did not need more money. I told her I had enough. The broker told me she had never heard of anyone saying they had enough money," said Grace.

"This all has to do with The Middle Path. A celibate on one extreme and a billionaire on the other. One is searching for enlightenment by subjecting herself or himself to a life of austerity and the other to a life of opulence. Each are craving something, and they will never find it as each of them, the one with nothing, and the one with everything cannot understand that they must be satisfied with what they have and not dissatisfied by cravings for what they want. For one, it is the craving for the illusive enlightenment never to be attained, and for the other the lust for money, the quest for things material ... more stuff. And they both suffer from the greatest dissatisfaction of all ... fear. The celibate has a fear of never being enlightened and the billionaire has the fear of losing it all. Both crave and cannot attain peace of mind ... they are out of their mind. The celibate will become a Guru and the billionaire will become richer, but they will never attain 'nirvana', which means 'to blow out' or 'to extinguish'. They cannot let go. They have trapped themselves."

"And this brings us to The Fourth Noble Truth. The Truth of the Path of the Cessation of Dissatisfaction. This path is within you. You are on that path as the ember ebbs. Through that path you can attain peace of mind.

There are eight 'rights' of the path. Those rights come from the eight-spoke wheel of Dharma, which means, 'the law'. This wheel has what you do, think, or say. The rights are in no particular order as the wheel keeps spinning."

"The Four Noble Truths and now the 'rights' of an eight-spoke wheel. How can I keep up with it all?" asked Grace.

"You will. It all fits together and when it comes together for you, you will understand The Buddha's teachings are the way to The Middle Path," said Zeus. "The eight 'rights' are: one, right action, protect, avoid causing harm; two, right livelihood, avoid being deceptive; three, right effort, present something positive instead of negativity; four, right view, follow The Four Noble Truths. Five is the right intention, which this is right thought that will take you away from dissatisfaction. Six is right mindfulness, this is staying in the now, and not dwelling on the past nor crave for something in the future. Seven is right concentration, keeping your reality free of distractions; and the eight is right speech, which means avoiding hurtful and idle talk. You can study more about these at your leisure. Then, there is the Wheel of Life. The wheel has three components. The first is the outer circle which shows us all the is suffering and dissatisfaction. There are 12," said Zeus.

"Again, with 12," said Grace.

"Yep, from Horus to The Buddha," replied Zeus.

"Amazing. I am ready for the 12," said Grace.

"I'll just give you the short version of the outer circle: ignorance, mental formations, name and form, sense bases, contact, feeling, craving, grasping, becoming, birth, aging and death, and consciousness."

Zeus continued, "In the second component there are root delusions and six realms of existence. One, there is the god realm, and two, anyone who wishes to be a god fears becoming a demi-god. Then, after those two comes number three, the animal realm which is the fourth, a notch below a human. Below the animal realm is the fifth realm which is the hungry ghosts. The hungry ghosts scratch out a living; but just barely. Then the sixth and last is the realm of the hell-beings. Hell-beings have nothing, and they suffer mental torment and physical agony. They live a tortured existence. This is the lowest of bad karma which we will discuss in a minute."

"In the inner-most portion of the wheel, the third component, rests the three greatest root delusions represented by a pig a rooster, and a snake. The pig represents ignorance. The rooster represents craving. And, the snake represents aversion; in this case schadenfreude."

"Above the wheel is a fierce figure holding the wheel which represents permanence. To the left of the wheel is the moon representing liberation. And, to the right of the wheel is The Buddha indicating that liberation is possible."

"Whew. That calls for a lot of studying," said Grace.

"Yes, it will, but if you can get away from the contrived 'miracles', you will find there is something there. Those who wrote the myths about The Buddha were, simply, trying to make a god out of him. The writing,

225

among other things tell of The Buddha being two persons: one in heaven with his mother and the other on the Earth. Then, it is written that The Buddha wanted to show his power to Buddhist monks. He created fireworks and then flew above them. The Buddha did not teach of gods, yet the writings put gods, yes plural, in the universe. For what reason. There is no explanation. Siddhartha's father, the king, sent ten couriers to Buddha. The first nine never returned but stayed with The Buddha. When the tenth courier arrived, The Buddha lifted into the sky where fire and water emanated from his body. This stuff, and I call it stuff is written in the Sutras which is Sanskrit for discourse. These 'scriptures' were written well after the death of The Buddha as I have mentioned before. Let me explain some definitions."

"Good, is Nirvana going to be explained?" asked Grace.

"Not just yet," said Zeus. "In order to understand Nirvana there are some other definitions for you to learn. You have heard of Karma? It is the sum of a person's actions in this and in previous states of existence, which is believed to decide their fate in future existences. It is sort of a reincarnated 'what comes around goes around'. How you live in this life, according to the laws of Karma, will have ramifications in the next life. This is where Buddhism runs off the rails."

"What do you mean? Does it have to do with the reincarnation thing?" asked Grace.

"Yes, the explanations I am about to give, have to do with that, with reincarnation," began Zeus. "Buddhism is a cycle of life, which is Karma; death, reincarnation, suffering, dissatisfaction, and striving for enlightenment. A simple answer to Karma is really not, what goes around, comes around. This is because Karma is not revenge of any sort. Instead, Karma is self-inflicted. Think about it."

"Then comes Samsara. Samsara is the cycle of death and rebirth in which life in the material world is bound. The Buddhist knows nothing of a past life. Do you remember what happened on the 10th of July 1880?"

"How could I remember. I was not yet born. Ah, so, how is one to prove the previous life. I can't, therefore it rests on faith alone. No proof," replied Grace.

"Next is Nirvana ..."

"Finally," said Grace.

"Nirvana is the final goal of Buddhism. It is when the believer is released from the cycle of death and rebirth. All suffering and dissatisfaction are extinguished. And, there is more after attaining Nirvana."

"Really?" said Grace.

"Yes, really," said Zeus. "It is being a Bodhisattva. A Bodhisattva is a person who has reached Nirvana but chooses to return through rebirth to save those still suffering. And the last is Nihilism, the final state of Buddhism. It is the rejection of all religious principles, often the belief that life has no meaning."

"Wait a minute. If that is true, why go through all of this religious mish-mash?" asked Grace.

"Mish-mash?" asked Zeus.

"Just a mess. Well, isn't it?" replied Grace.

"Is it possible that nothingness is death to the enlightened Buddhist?" asked Zeus.

"Perhaps, we all become enlightened with the last breath?" replied Grace.

"Correct. That would be the Uncaused Cause or the First Cause interfering in the universe. The First Cause does not interfere nor has First Cause any influence in the creation that takes its natural course. There is no after-life. Death is the course of nature. The ember has burned out, has it not?" asked Zeus.

"Yes, it is all beginning to come together for me." replied Grace.

"Do you feel this is a good place for you to finally be free?" asked Zeus.

"Yes, and I am surprised that the freedom would come from hearing about Buddhism. It's a matter of remaining open to new concepts, " replied Grace.

"It overcomes you all at once. Buddhism, without all of those made-up miracles, can help people on a path to enlightenment. But, they have got to come clean. Just as you, have. You are now enlightened as the freedom from religion has set you on a course of happiness. Robert Green Ingersoll wrote ..."

"He is the agnostic?"

"Correct," said Zeus. "He wrote, 'While I am opposed to all orthodox creeds, I have a creed myself; and my creed is this. Happiness is the only good. The time to be happy is now. The place to be happy is here. The way to be happy is to make others so. The creed is somewhat short, but is long *enough for this life, strong enough for this world. If there is another world, when we get there we can make another creed'."*

"What a beautiful, simple way to explain how we are meant to live. It's something that I want to memorize, to always have the words with me," said Grace.

"Good idea," said Zeus. "I must leave you now."

"So, what is our topic for tomorrow night?" asked Grace.

"We are going to discuss ... nah ... I'll keep you in suspense," said Zeus

"Oh, don't do that," replied Grace.

"Got to," laughed Zeus. "Night."

"If you must. Good night."

CHAPTER TWENTY-ONE

THEN GRACE WAS GONE

"Grace. I have good news for you," said Thelma. "Have a seat."

"Am I being sprung?" laughed Grace.

"Yes. And although I hate to see you go, I hope you, never again, have a need to return," replied Thelma.

"I don't think I will be coming back. I will miss the entire staff on the ladies' floor, but especially you. And, Doctor Phelps, also," said Grace. "When I first arrived, I had so many questions, and so much doubt about myself. As I look at my stay, I realize it was a journey into the unknown that has given me a new outlook about so many things. I no longer am amazed at my new understanding."

"What's your new understanding," asked Thelma

"For me, and for my belief system all of my life," started Grace. "I now realize has been based on fear. Mostly, fear that if I did not live a good life or if I did something really horrible while living, I would not go to heaven. No, I was taught that I would end up in hell, forever...for eternity."

"I never looked at it being fear-based, but when you put it that way, yes, I guess that was the way I was raised...the way most of my family has been raised," said Thelma.

"Maybe by asking you a question I've repeatedly asked myself, it will provide some insight to my understanding. What is the point in God condemning men, women and children to an afterlife of living in hell?"

"So that we'll live a good life and be good to others…to go to heaven," said Thelma.

"I don't believe that, anymore. I'll give you a simple example. What about the Jewish girl who is raped and eventually killed by the soldier who calls himself a Christian? Is she condemned to live her afterlife of eternity in hell because she is Jewish and not Christian after being defiled by a Christian?"

"You're talking of the holocaust. Right?" asked Thelma.

"That's right. Plus, about all of the genocides that have been done in the name of God. Of all the injustices of man's inhumanity to man, in the name of God," said Grace.

"But, are you saying you don't believe in God anymore because of these injustices?" asked Thelma.

No, that's not the understanding. Not at all. The understanding is that it is religion that causes us to behave the way we do. We fight wars, we find fault with others, we treat others with disdain, not in the name of God, but rather, in the name of religion. Religion does not and has never provided the solution to living a good life. More often, proven by centuries of horrible things being done to others to get people to believe in a certain religion, it has provided the reason for war and for genocide," replied Grace.

"So, does that mean you want all religions to go away?" asked Thelma.

"Grace replied, "No, not at all. This won't provide a solution in the near future, either. People need religion, need their faith."

"Then, what is your understanding?"

"Simply put, understand what you believe, avoiding believing because of fear," replied Grace.

"When did you come to this realization?" asked Thelma.

"I've been working on this since before I came here, and it has become clearer and clearer to me with last night being the real turning point," replied Grace.

What happened last night?

"I learned about the Four Noble Truths. That is, the truths of suffering, the cause of suffering, the cessation of cause of suffering and finally, the path to the cessation of the cause of suffering," said Grace.

"All that sounds very confusing. And, also, it all sounds the same," replied Thelma.

"I suppose so. But, for me, for now, these premises finally provide me peace. For me, living is in the now and I no longer cling on the premise of going to heaven or to hell based on how I live while here on earth," said Grace.

I have seen a lot of recoveries over the years in my work here. But, I can honestly say, I have never seen one quite like yours. You say you've learned this all by hearing a voice. Right?" asked Thelma.

"Yes, his name is Zeus," replied Grace.

"It does sound like you do have peace," said Thelma.

Yes, finally," replied Grace.

"Give me a hug. Doctor Phelps is releasing you to go home tomorrow morning. A car service will be here for you at nine to take you to Logan," said Thelma.

"Best hug ever," said Grace. "You never judged. Thank-you for that,"

"No Grace, I never did. I have known what you have discovered for quite some time. I understand your peace and am grateful you found it. Love, and all the best to you," said Thelma.

<<<>>>

"Grace. Grace

Zeus. Zeus. What am I going to learn tonight?" asked Grace.

"Well Grace, I think we have just about covered what I hoped to teach you. Do you have an ember, anymore?" asked Zeus.

"No, not anymore," said Grace. "I was surprised. I thought I would feel ... well ... different."

"How do you mean?" asked Zeus.

"I felt that it would probably be a let-down, that I would be giving up something that had meant so much to me for so long. I thought it would feel as if someone had died," replied Grace.

"It doesn't though, does it? The ember no longer lingers. That's because you have made the trip with each new stop having a true understanding.

Although you kept talking about the ember, I think you knew all along you were finally ready for the truth. You would not have heard me if you were not ready for the journey. Plus, you didn't have to do it alone, either. We did it together." said Zeus.

"Thank-you for coming into my life, to take me on this wonderful journey," replied Grace. "When I first arrived, I was so disillusioned and so depressed. And the guilt! I could not let go of the feeling I had turned my back on something I have lived with all my life. That scared me because I did not know what I would replace it with … now … it seems so simple, so logical … so, in the now."

"In the now. What does the now 'look' like to you? 'Feel' like to you?" asked Zeus.

"First and most profound to me," began Grace. "… I don't feel guilty anymore. That is a huge step for me. I am more at peace with myself and my new understanding of religion, faith, and belief, than at any other time in my life. Traveling with you … well … you have brought me along, to this point, with logic, and through … I guess I can say … examples … contradictions … of my former religion as well as other religions."

"So, what now? Have you given any thought to what you want to do with your new knowledge? Or, is it too soon?" asked Zeus.

"The best way for me to answer those questions is with a yes and a no. The one thing I know, with all that I have learned from you, and learned about myself as we traveled on our journey … well … I have no plans to ever 'preach' again. There is nothing to be gained to preach what I have learned.

It can't be taught. It has to be experienced ... learned. Others must learn in their own way, in their own time. I guess you are ready for your next student," said Grace.

"Yes, there is always someone who needs that little push towards the truth. As for you, how about you teaching what you have learned on your journey? Wouldn't you like others to feel the freedom you have ... in the now?" asked Zeus.

"I found peace with you, because I was ready to find the answers. As for my former peers or the rest of the world, hopefully, in time, they will be receptive and hear. I don't think it wise or even fair to take away from them what they have faith in and believe. Creating such a void would be cruel. It could cause so much needless pain. For now, religion has an important place in their lives," said Grace.

"Those are wise words," began Zeus. "And, I am grateful I have given you that understanding and that you have come to that conclusion. You have learned more than what I could have taught you ... you were perceptive."

"Yes, I can now call myself a Deist. I am sane enough and humane enough to believe in the existence ... no ... not belief ... but have an understanding in the existence of a supreme being, specifically a creator, who does not intervene in the universe. And, for that very reason, knowing what Deism holds as a truth the universal path of 'live and let live'," said Grace.

"You have come full circle. You are not insane ... you are not crazy ... you are not an agnostic ... nor an atheist ... you came here to find yourself," replied Zeus.

"I must admit though, I am somewhat saddened by what I now know, from what you have taught me about my former religion and the religions of others," said Grace.

"Although I think I know the answer 'why', could you tell me please?" asked Zeus.

"All knowing Zeus. You do know," said Grace. "As long as there are different religions in the world, each with their own god, and as long as each religion continues to have its own set of rules and covenants, the world will never know peace. It is just the very nature of religious beliefs. All religions teach if one person does not believe the way of another person, that other person is not godly or worse, not equal."

"Yes, the Catholics have separate cemeteries for their dead. And, unless a Catholic has confessed sins to a priest ... well ... communion is out of the question," said Zeus.

"I remember the first tenet of Roman Catholicism ... if you are not a repentant Catholic ... well ... you don't go to heaven," said Grace.

"And Mormons, unless a Mormon, one is not allowed into their temples and meeting houses. Strangers are distained, for their covenants are different, therefore not equal," said Zeus.

"And, as with me, when I was a preacher, as long as Christian clergy continued to read only the 'good parts' of the Bible to their flocks, those in the flocks felt good when they left the church on Sunday. The denial of what is so much of the Bible is nothing but hypocrisy," said Grace. "All in the name of god."

"That is right. All in the name of god. So, again, what do you plan to do with your life now that the ember is burned out?" asked Zeus

"I am not afraid of the truth anymore. If I help someone here and there along the way to also find their peace, I feel I will, again, have a purpose. And, those that cannot nor will not see the obvious. If they elect to remain as they are, in deep doubt, that too, is alright," replied Grace."

"Grace, you have a wonderful plan and for obvious reasons I am pleased that you have accepted this as your new 'calling'. I was hopeful that you would eventually be comfortable with your Deism. I couldn't be more pleased that you now have a new direction. It has been a pleasure, a delight, and an honor, to have been your 'voice' all these nights you have been open to hearing me. There is no more I can do for you than to wish you nothing but the best," said Zeus.

"Thank-you, hardly seems enough to say to you, but I know, you know, how I really feel. I am very grateful. I will cherish our nights together and will always remember this wonderful, enlightening, journey. Good night, Zeus, my loving god of ages past."

"And pleasant dreams Grace. Good bye."

Fin

Made in the USA
Columbia, SC
07 November 2018